CRAZY MEDITERRANEAN 2022

DELICIOUS AND SUPERTASTY RECIPES

SAM BELL

Table of Contents

Chicken Fiesta Salad 9

Corn & Black Bean Salad 11

Awesome Pasta Salad 12

Tuna Salad 14

Southern Potato Salad 15

Seven-Layer Salad 17

Kale, Quinoa & Avocado Salad with Lemon Dijon Vinaigrette 19

Chicken Salad 21

Cobb Salad 23

Broccoli Salad 25

Strawberry Spinach Salad 27

Pear Salad with Roquefort Cheese 29

Mexican Bean Salad 31

Melon Salad 33

Orange Celery Salad 35

Roasted Broccoli Salad 36

Tomato Salad 38

Feta Beet Salad 39

Cauliflower & Tomato Salad 40

Pilaf with Cream Cheese 41

Roasted Eggplant Salad 43

Roasted Veggies 44

Pistachio Arugula Salad 46

Parmesan Barley Risotto 47

Seafood & Avocado Salad	49
Mediterranean Shrimp Salad	51
Chickpea Pasta Salad	52
Mediterranean Stir Fry	54
Balsamic Cucumber Salad	56
Beef Kefta Patties with Cucumber Salad	57
Chicken and Cucumber Salad with Parsley Pesto	59
Easy Arugula Salad	61
Feta Garbanzo Bean Salad	62
Greek Brown and Wild Rice Bowls	63
Greek Dinner Salad	64
Halibut with Lemon-Fennel Salad	66
Herbed Greek Chicken Salad	68
Greek Couscous Salad	70
Denver Fried Omelet	72
Sausage Pan	74
Grilled Marinated Shrimp	76
Sausage Egg Casserole	78
Baked Omelet Squares	80
Hard-Boiled Egg	82
Mushrooms with a Soy Sauce Glaze	83
Egg Cupcakes	85
Dinosaur Eggs	87
Paleo Almond Banana Pancakes	91
Zucchini with Egg	93
Cheesy Amish Breakfast Casserole	94
Salad with Roquefort Cheese	96

Rice with Vermicelli 98
Fava Beans and Rice 100
Buttered Fava Beans 102
Freekeh 103
Fried Rice Balls with Tomato Sauce 104
Spanish-Style Rice 106
Zucchini with Rice and Tzatziki 108
Cannellini Beans with Rosemary and Garlic Aioli 110
Jeweled Rice 111
Asparagus Risotto 113
Moroccan Tagine with Vegetables 115
Chickpea Lettuce Wraps with Celery 117
Grilled Vegetable Skewers 118
Stuffed Portobello Mushroom with Tomatoes 120
Wilted Dandelion Greens with Sweet Onion 122
Celery and Mustard Greens 123
Vegetable and Tofu Scramble 124
Simple Zoodles 126
Lentil and Tomato Collard Wraps 127
Mediterranean Veggie Bowl 129
Grilled Veggie and Hummus Wrap 131
Spanish Green Beans 133
Rustic Cauliflower and Carrot Hash 134
Roasted Cauliflower and Tomatoes 135
Roasted Acorn Squash 137
Sautéed Garlic Spinach 139
Garlicky Sautéed Zucchini with Mint 140

Stewed Okra 141
Sweet Veggie-Stuffed Peppers 142
Moussaka Eggplant 144
Vegetable-Stuffed Grape Leaves 146
Grilled Eggplant Rolls 148
Crispy Zucchini Fritters 150
Cheesy Spinach Pies 152
Cucumber Sandwich Bites 154
Yogurt Dip 155
Tomato Bruschetta 156
Olives and Cheese Stuffed Tomatoes 158
Pepper Tapenade 159
Coriander Falafel 160
Red Pepper Hummus 162
White Bean Dip 163
Hummus with Ground Lamb 164
Eggplant Dip 165
Veggie Fritters 166
Bulgur Lamb Meatballs 168
Cucumber Bites 170
Stuffed Avocado 171
Wrapped Plums 172
Marinated Feta and Artichokes 173
Tuna Croquettes 174
Smoked Salmon Crudités 176
Citrus-Marinated Olives 177
Olive Tapenade with Anchovies 178

Greek Deviled Eggs 180

Manchego Crackers 182

Burrata Caprese Stack 184

Zucchini-Ricotta Fritters with Lemon-Garlic Aioli 185

Salmon-Stuffed Cucumbers 187

Goat Cheese–Mackerel Pâté 188

Taste of the Mediterranean Fat Bombs 190

Avocado Gazpacho 191

Crab Cake Lettuce Cups 193

Orange-Tarragon Chicken Salad Wrap 195

Feta and Quinoa Stuffed Mushrooms 197

Five-Ingredient Falafel with Garlic-Yogurt Sauce 199

Lemon Shrimp with Garlic Olive Oil 201

Crispy Green Bean Fries with Lemon-Yogurt Sauce 203

Homemade Sea Salt Pita Chips 205

Baked Spanakopita Dip 206

Roasted Pearl Onion Dip 208

Red Pepper Tapenade 210

Greek Potato Skins with Olives and Feta 212

Artichoke and Olive Pita Flatbread 214

Mini Crab Cakes 216

Zucchini Feta Roulades 218

Chicken Fiesta Salad

Preparation Time : 20 minutes

Cooking Time : 20 minutes

Servings : 4

Difficulty Level : Easy

Ingredients:

- 2 halves of chicken fillet without skin or bones
- 1 packet of herbs for fajitas, divided
- 1 tablespoon vegetable oil
- 1 can black beans, rinsed and drained
- 1 box of Mexican-style corn
- 1/2 cup of salsa
- 1 packet of green salad
- 1 onion, minced
- 1 tomato, quartered

Directions:

Rub the chicken evenly with 1/2 of the herbs for fajitas. Cook the oil in a frying pan over medium heat and cook the chicken for 8 minutes on the side by side or until the juice is clear; put aside. Combine beans, corn, salsa, and other 1/2 fajita spices in a large pan. Heat over medium heat until lukewarm. Prepare the salad by mixing green vegetables, onion, and tomato. Cover the chicken salad and dress the beans and corn mixture.

Nutrition (for 100g): 311 calories 6.4g fat 42.2g carbohydrates 23g protein 853mg sodium

Corn & Black Bean Salad

Preparation Time : 10 minutes
Cooking Time : 0 minutes
Servings : 4
Difficulty Level : Easy

Ingredients:

- 2 tablespoons vegetable oil
- 1/4 cup balsamic vinegar
- 1/2 teaspoon of salt
- 1/2 teaspoon of white sugar
- 1/2 teaspoon ground cumin
- 1/2 teaspoon ground black pepper
- 1/2 teaspoon chili powder
- 3 tablespoons chopped fresh coriander
- 1 can black beans (15 oz)
- 1 can of sweetened corn (8.75 oz) drained

Directions:

Combine balsamic vinegar, oil, salt, sugar, black pepper, cumin and chili powder in a small bowl. Combine black corn and beans in a medium bowl. Mix with vinegar and oil vinaigrette and garnish with coriander. Cover and refrigerate overnight.

Nutrition (for 100g): 214 calories 8.4 g fat 28.6g carbohydrates 7.5g protein 415mg sodium

Awesome Pasta Salad

Preparation Time : 30 minutes

Cooking Time : 10 minutes

Servings : 16

Difficulty Level : Average

Ingredients:

- 1 (16-oz) fusilli pasta package
- 3 cups of cherry tomatoes
- 1/2 pound of provolone, diced
- 1/2 pound of sausage, diced
- 1/4 pound of pepperoni, cut in half
- 1 large green pepper
- 1 can of black olives, drained
- 1 jar of chilis, drained
- 1 bottle (8 oz) Italian vinaigrette

Directions:

Boil a lightly salted water in a pot. Stir in the pasta and cook for about 8 to 10 minutes or until al dente. Drain and rinse with cold water.

Combine pasta with tomatoes, cheese, salami, pepperoni, green pepper, olives, and peppers in a large bowl. Pour the vinaigrette and mix well.

Nutrition (for 100g): 310 calories 17.7g fat 25.9g carbohydrates 12.9g protein 746mg sodium

Tuna Salad

Preparation Time : 20 minutes
Cooking Time : 0 minutes
Servings : 4
Difficulty Level : Easy

Ingredients:

- 1 (19 ounce) can of garbanzo beans
- 2 tablespoons mayonnaise
- 2 teaspoons of spicy brown mustard
- 1 tablespoon sweet pickle
- Salt and pepper to taste
- 2 chopped green onions

Directions:

Combine green beans, mayonnaise, mustard, sauce, chopped green onions, salt and pepper in a medium bowl. Mix well.

Nutrition (for 100g): 220 calories 7.2g fat 32.7g carbohydrates 7g protein 478mg sodium

Southern Potato Salad

Preparation Time : 15 minutes
Cooking Time : 15 minutes
Servings : 4
Difficulty Level : Average

Ingredients:

- 4 potatoes
- 4 eggs
- 1/2 stalk of celery, finely chopped
- 1/4 cup sweet taste
- 1 clove of garlic minced
- 2 tablespoons mustard
- 1/2 cup mayonnaise
- salt and pepper to taste

Directions:

Boil water in a pot then situate the potatoes and cook until soft but still firm, about 15 minutes; drain and chop. Transfer the eggs in a pan and cover with cold water.

Boil the water; cover, remove from heat, and let the eggs soak in hot water for 10 minutes. Remove then shell and chop.

Combine potatoes, eggs, celery, sweet sauce, garlic, mustard, mayonnaise, salt, and pepper in a large bowl. Mix and serve hot.

Nutrition (for 100g): 460 calories 27.4g fat 44.6g carbohydrates 11.3g protein 214mg sodium

Seven-Layer Salad

Preparation Time : 15 minutes
Cooking Time : 5 minutes
Servings : 10
Difficulty Level : Average

Ingredients:

- 1-pound bacon
- 1 head iceberg lettuce
- 1 red onion, minced
- 1 pack of 10 frozen peas, thawed
- 10 oz grated cheddar cheese
- 1 cup chopped cauliflower
- 1 1/4 cup mayonnaise
- 2 tablespoons white sugar
- 2/3 cup grated Parmesan cheese

Directions:

Put the bacon in a huge, shallow frying pan. Bake over medium heat until smooth. Crumble and set aside. Situate the chopped lettuce in a large bowl and cover with a layer of an onion, peas, grated cheese, cauliflower, and bacon.

Prepare the vinaigrette by mixing the mayonnaise, sugar, and parmesan cheese. Pour over the salad and cool to cool.

Nutrition (for 100g): 387 calories 32.7g fat 9.9g carbohydrates 14.5g protein 609mg sodium

Kale, Quinoa & Avocado Salad with Lemon Dijon Vinaigrette

Preparation Time : 5 minutes
Cooking Time : 25 minutes
Servings : 4
Difficulty Level : Difficult

Ingredients:

- 2/3 cup of quinoa
- 1 1/3 cup of water
- 1 bunch of kale, torn into bite-sized pieces
- 1/2 avocado - peeled, diced and pitted
- 1/2 cup chopped cucumber
- 1/3 cup chopped red pepper
- 2 tablespoons chopped red onion
- 1 tablespoon of feta crumbled

Directions:

Boil the quinoa and 1 1/3 cup of water in a pan. Adjust heat and simmer until quinoa is tender and water is absorbed for about 15 to 20 minutes. Set aside to cool.

Place the cabbage in a steam basket over more than an inch of boiling water in a pan. Seal the pan with a lid and steam until hot, about 45 seconds; transfer to a large plate. Garnish with cabbage, quinoa, avocado, cucumber, pepper, red onion, and feta cheese.

Combine olive oil, lemon juice, Dijon mustard, sea salt, and black pepper in a bowl until the oil is emulsified in the dressing; pour over the salad.

Nutrition (for 100g): 342 calories 20.3g fat 35.4g carbohydrates 8.9g protein 705mg sodium

Chicken Salad

Preparation Time : 20 minutes
Cooking Time : 0 minutes
Servings : 9
Difficulty Level : Easy

Ingredients:

- 1/2 cup mayonnaise
- 1/2 teaspoon of salt
- 3/4 teaspoon of poultry herbs
- 1 tablespoon lemon juice
- 3 cups cooked chicken breast, diced
- 1/4 teaspoon ground black pepper
- 1/4 teaspoon garlic powder
- 1/4 teaspoon onion powder
- 1/2 cup finely chopped celery
- 1 (8 oz) box of water chestnuts, drained and chopped
- 1/2 cup chopped green onions
- 1 1/2 cups green grapes cut in half
- 1 1/2 cups diced Swiss cheese

Directions:

Combine mayonnaise, salt, chicken spices, onion powder, garlic powder, pepper, and lemon juice in a medium bowl. Combine chicken, celery, green onions, water chestnuts, Swiss cheese, and raisins in a big bowl. Stir in the mayonnaise mixture and coat. Cool until ready to serve.

Nutrition (for 100g): 293 calories 19.5g fat 10.3g carbohydrates 19.4g protein 454mg sodium

Cobb Salad

Preparation Time : 5 minutes
Cooking Time : 15 minutes
Servings : 6
Difficulty Level : Difficult

Ingredients:

- 6 slices of bacon
- 3 eggs
- 1 cup Iceberg lettuce, grated
- 3 cups cooked minced chicken meat
- 2 tomatoes, seeded and minced
- 3/4 cup of blue cheese, crumbled
- 1 avocado - peeled, pitted and diced
- 3 green onions, minced
- 1 bottle (8 oz.) Ranch Vinaigrette

Directions:

Situate the eggs in a pan and soak them completely with cold water. Boil the water. Cover and remove from heat and let the eggs rest in hot water for 10 to 12 minutes. Remove from hot water, let cool, peel, and chop. Situate the bacon in a big, deep frying pan. Bake over medium heat until smooth. Set aside.

Divide the grated lettuce into separate plates. Spread chicken, eggs, tomatoes, blue cheese, bacon, avocado, and green onions in rows on lettuce. Sprinkle with your favorite vinaigrette and enjoy.

Nutrition (for 100g): 525 calories 39.9g fat 10.2g carbohydrates 31.7g protein 701mg sodium

Broccoli Salad

Preparation Time : 10 minutes

Cooking Time : 15 minutes

Servings : 6

Difficulty Level : Average

Ingredients:

- 10 slices of bacon
- 1 cup fresh broccoli
- ¼ cup red onion, minced
- ½ cup raisins
- 3 tablespoons white wine vinegar
- 2 tablespoons white sugar
- 1 cup mayonnaise
- 1 cup of sunflower seeds

Directions:

Cook the bacon in a deep-frying pan over medium heat. Drain, crumble, and set aside. Combine broccoli, onion, and raisins in a medium bowl. Mix vinegar, sugar, and mayonnaise in a small bowl. Pour over the broccoli mixture and mix. Cool for at least two hours.

Before serving, mix the salad with crumbled bacon and sunflower seeds.

Nutrition (for 100g): 559 calories 48.1g fat 31g carbohydrates 18g protein 584mg sodium

Strawberry Spinach Salad

Preparation Time : 10 minutes

Cooking Time : 0 minutes

Servings : 4

Difficulty Level : Easy

Ingredients:

- 2 tablespoons sesame seeds
- 1 tablespoon poppy seeds
- 1/2 cup white sugar
- 1/2 cup olive oil
- 1/4 cup distilled white vinegar
- 1/4 teaspoon paprika
- 1/4 teaspoon Worcestershire sauce
- 1 tablespoon minced onion
- 10 ounces fresh spinach
- 1-quart strawberries - cleaned, hulled and sliced
- 1/4 cup almonds, blanched and slivered

Directions:

In a medium bowl, whisk together the same seeds, poppy seeds, sugar, olive oil, vinegar, paprika, Worcestershire sauce, and onion. Cover, and chill for one hour.

In a large bowl, incorporate the spinach, strawberries, and almonds. Drizzle dressing over salad and toss. Refrigerate 10 to 15 minutes before serving.

Nutrition (for 100g): 491 calories 35.2g fat 42.9g carbohydrates 6g protein 691mg sodium

Pear Salad with Roquefort Cheese

Preparation Time : 20 minutes

Cooking Time : 10 minutes

Servings : 2

Difficulty Level : Average

Ingredients:

- 1 leaf lettuce, torn into bite-sized pieces
- 3 pears - peeled, cored and diced
- 5 ounces Roquefort, crumbled
- 1 avocado - peeled, seeded and diced
- 1/2 cup chopped green onions
- 1/4 cup white sugar
- 1/2 cup pecan nuts
- 1/3 cup olive oil
- 3 tablespoons red wine vinegar
- 1 1/2 teaspoon of white sugar
- 1 1/2 teaspoon of prepared mustard
- 1/2 teaspoon of salted black pepper
- 1 clove of garlic

Directions:

Stir in 1/4 cup of sugar with the pecans in a pan over medium heat. Continue to stir gently until the sugar caramelized with pecans. Cautiously transfer the nuts to wax paper. Let it chill and break into pieces.

Mix for vinaigrette oil, marinade, 1 1/2 teaspoon of sugar, mustard, chopped garlic, salt, and pepper.

In a deep bowl, combine lettuce, pears, blue cheese, avocado, and green onions. Put vinaigrette over salad, sprinkle with pecans and serve.

Nutrition (for 100g): 426 calories 31.6g fat 33.1g carbohydrates 8g protein 481mg sodium

Mexican Bean Salad

Preparation Time : 15 minutes
Cooking Time : 0 minutes
Servings : 6
Difficulty Level : Easy

Ingredients:

- 1 can black beans (15 oz), drained
- 1 can red beans (15 oz), drained
- 1 can white beans (15 oz), drained
- 1 green pepper, minced
- 1 red pepper, minced
- 1 pack of frozen corn kernels
- 1 red onion, minced
- 2 tablespoons fresh lime juice
- 1/2 cup olive oil
- 1/2 cup red wine vinegar
- 1 tablespoon lemon juice
- 1 tablespoon salt
- 2 tablespoons white sugar
- 1 clove of crushed garlic
- 1/4 cup chopped coriander
- 1/2 tablespoon ground cumin
- 1/2 tablespoon ground black pepper
- 1 dash of hot pepper sauce

- 1/2 teaspoon chili powder

Directions:

Combine beans, peppers, frozen corn, and red onion in a large bowl. Combine olive oil, lime juice, red wine vinegar, lemon juice, sugar, salt, garlic, coriander, cumin, and black pepper in a small bowl — season with hot sauce and chili powder.

Pour the vinaigrette with olive oil over the vegetables; mix well. Cool well and serve cold.

Nutrition (for 100g): 334 calories 14.8g fat 41.7g carbohydrates 11.2g protein 581mg sodium

Melon Salad

Preparation Time : 20 minutes
Cooking Time : 0 minutes
Servings : 6
Difficulty Level : Average

Ingredients:

- ¼ teaspoon sea salt
- ¼ teaspoon black pepper
- 1 tablespoon balsamic vinegar
- 1 cantaloupe, quartered & seeded
- 12 watermelon, small & seedless
- 2 cups mozzarella balls, fresh
- 1/3 cup basil, fresh & torn
- 2 tbsp. olive oil

Directions:

Scrape out balls of cantaloupe, and the place them in a colander over a serving bowl. Use your melon baller to cut the watermelon as well, and then put them in with your cantaloupe.

Allow your fruit to drain for ten minutes, and then refrigerate the juice for another recipe. It can even be added to smoothies. Wipe the bowl dry, and then place your fruit in it.

Add in your basil, oil, vinegar, mozzarella and tomatoes before seasoning with salt and pepper. Gently mix and serve immediately or chilled.

Nutrition (for 100g): 218 Calories 13g Fat 9g Carbohydrates 10g Protein 581mg Sodium

Orange Celery Salad

Preparation Time : 15 minutes

Cooking Time : 0 minutes

Servings : 6

Difficulty Level : Easy

Ingredients:

- 1 tablespoon lemon juice, fresh
- ¼ teaspoon sea salt, fine
- ¼ teaspoon black pepper
- 1 tablespoon olive brine
- 1 tablespoon olive oil
- ¼ cup red onion, sliced
- ½ cup green olives
- 2 oranges, peeled & sliced
- 3 celery stalks, sliced diagonally in ½ inch slices

Directions:

Put your oranges, olives, onion and celery in a shallow bowl. In a different bowl whisk your oil, olive brine and lemon juice, pour this over your salad. Season with salt and pepper before serving.

Nutrition (for 100g): 65 Calories 7g Fats 9g Carbohydrates 2g Protein 614mg Sodium

Roasted Broccoli Salad

Preparation Time : 20 minutes

Cooking Time : 10 minutes

Servings : 4

Difficulty Level : Difficult

Ingredients:

- 1 lb. broccoli, cut into florets & stem sliced
- 3 tablespoons olive oil, divided
- 1-pint cherry tomatoes
- 1 ½ teaspoons honey, raw & divided
- 3 cups cubed bread, whole grain
- 1 tablespoon balsamic vinegar
- ½ teaspoon black pepper
- ¼ teaspoon sea salt, fine
- grated parmesan for serving

Directions:

Prepare oven at 450 degrees, and then get out a rimmed baking sheet. Place it in the oven to heat up. Drizzle your broccoli with a tablespoon of oil, and toss to coat.

Remove the baking sheet form the oven, and spoon the broccoli on it. Leave oil it eh bottom of the bowl, add in your tomatoes, toss to coat, and then toss your tomatoes with a tablespoon of honey. Pour them on the same baking sheet as your broccoli.

Roast for fifteen minutes, and stir halfway through your cooking time. Add in your bread, and then roast for three more minutes. Whisk two tablespoons of oil, vinegar, and remaining honey. Season with salt and pepper. Pour this over your broccoli mix to serve.

Nutrition (for 100g): 226 Calories 12g Fat 26g Carbohydrates 7g Protein 581mg Sodium

Tomato Salad

Preparation Time : 20 minutes
Cooking Time : 0 minutes
Servings : 4
Difficulty Level : Easy

Ingredients:

- 1 cucumber, sliced
- ¼ cup sun dried tomatoes, chopped
- 1 lb. tomatoes, cubed
- ½ cup black olives
- 1 red onion, sliced
- 1 tablespoon balsamic vinegar
- ¼ cup parsley, fresh & chopped
- 2 tablespoons olive oil
- sea salt & black pepper to taste

Directions:

Get out a bowl and combine all of your vegetables together. To make your dressing mix all your seasoning, olive oil and vinegar. Toss with your salad and serve fresh.

Nutrition (for 100g): 126 Calories 9.2g Fat 11.5g Carbohydrates 2.1g Protein 681mg Sodium

Feta Beet Salad

Preparation Time : 15 minutes

Cooking Time : 0 minutes

Servings : 4

Difficulty Level : Easy

Ingredients:

- 6 red beets, cooked & peeled
- 3 ounces feta cheese, cubed
- 2 tablespoons olive oil
- 2 tablespoons balsamic vinegar

Directions:

Combine everything together, and then serve.

Nutrition (for 100g): 230 Calories 12g Fat 26.3g Carbohydrates 7.3g Protein 614mg Sodium

Cauliflower & Tomato Salad

Preparation Time : 15 minutes
Cooking Time : 0 minutes
Servings : 4
Difficulty Level : Easy

Ingredients:

- 1 head cauliflower, chopped
- 2 tablespoons parsley, fresh & chopped
- 2 cups cherry tomatoes, halved
- 2 tablespoons lemon juice, fresh
- 2 tablespoons pine nuts
- sea salt & black pepper to taste

Directions:

Mix your lemon juice, cherry tomatoes, cauliflower and parsley together, and then season. Top with pine nuts, and mix well before serving.

Nutrition (for 100g): 64 Calories 3.3g Fat 7.9g Carbohydrates 2.8g Protein 614mg Sodium

Pilaf with Cream Cheese

Preparation Time : 20 minutes

Cooking Time : 10 minutes

Servings : 6

Difficulty Level : Average

Ingredients:

- 2 cups yellow long grain rice, parboiled
- 1 cup onion
- 4 green onions
- 3 tablespoons butter
- 3 tablespoons vegetable broth
- 2 teaspoons cayenne pepper
- 1 teaspoon paprika
- ½ teaspoon cloves, minced
- 2 tablespoons mint leaves, fresh & chopped
- 1 bunch fresh mint leaves to garnish
- 1 tablespoons olive oil
- sea salt & black pepper to taste
- <u>Cheese Cream:</u>
- 3 tablespoons olive oil
- sea salt & black pepper to taste
- 9 ounces cream cheese

Directions:

Ready the oven at 360 degrees, and then pull out a pan. Heat your butter and olive oil together, and cook your onions and spring onions for two minutes.

Add in your salt, pepper, paprika, cloves, vegetable broth, rice and remaining seasoning. Sauté for three minutes. Wrap with foil, and bake for another half hour. Allow it to cool.

Mix in the cream cheese, cheese, olive oil, salt and pepper. Serve your pilaf garnished with fresh mint leaves.

Nutrition (for 100g): 364 Calories 30g Fat 20g Carbohydrates 5g Protein 511mg Sodium

Roasted Eggplant Salad

Preparation Time : 10 minutes
Cooking Time : 20 minutes
Servings : 6
Difficulty Level : Easy

Ingredients:

- 1 red onion, sliced
- 2 tablespoons parsley, fresh & chopped
- 1 teaspoon thyme
- 2 cups cherry tomatoes, halved
- sea salt & black pepper to taste
- 1 teaspoon oregano
- 3 tablespoons olive oil
- 1 teaspoon basil
- 3 eggplants, peeled & cubed

Directions:

Start by heating your oven to 350. Season your eggplant with basil, salt, pepper, oregano, thyme and olive oil. Situate it on a baking tray, and bake for a half hour. Toss with your remaining ingredients before serving.

Nutrition (for 100g): 148 Calories 7.7g Fat 20.5g Carbohydrates 3.5g Protein 660mg Sodium

Roasted Veggies

Preparation Time : 5 minutes

Cooking Time : 15 minutes

Servings : 12

Difficulty Level : Easy

Ingredients:

- 6 cloves garlic
- 6 tablespoons olive oil
- 1 fennel bulb, diced
- 1 zucchini, diced
- 2 red bell peppers, diced
- 6 potatoes, large & diced
- 2 teaspoons sea salt
- ½ cup balsamic vinegar
- ¼ cup rosemary, chopped & fresh
- 2 teaspoons vegetable bouillon powder

Directions:

Start by heating your oven to 400. Put your potatoes, fennel, zucchini, garlic and fennel on a baking dish, drizzling with olive oil. Sprinkle with salt, bouillon powder, and rosemary. Mix well, and then bake at 450 for thirty to forty minutes. Mix your vinegar into the vegetables before serving.

Nutrition (for 100g): 675 Calories 21g Fat 112g Carbohydrates 13g Protein 718mg Sodium

Pistachio Arugula Salad

Preparation Time : 20 minutes
Cooking Time : 0 minutes
Servings : 6
Difficulty Level : Easy

Ingredients:

- 6 cups kale, chopped
- ¼ cup olive oil
- 2 tablespoons lemon juice, fresh
- ½ teaspoon smoked paprika
- 2 cups arugula
- 1/3 cup pistachios, unsalted & shelled
- 6 tablespoons parmesan cheese, grated

Directions:

Get out a salad bowl and combine your oil, lemon, smoked paprika and kale. Gently massage the leaves for half a minute. Your kale should be coated well. Gently mix your arugula and pistachios when ready to serve.

Nutrition (for 100g): 150 Calories 12g Fat 8g Carbohydrates 5g Protein 637mg Sodium

Parmesan Barley Risotto

Preparation Time : 10 minutes
Cooking Time : 20 minutes
Servings : 6
Difficulty Level : Difficult

Ingredients:

- 1 cup yellow onion, chopped
- 1 tablespoon olive oil
- 4 cups vegetable broth, low sodium
- 2 cups pearl barley, uncooked
- ½ cup dry white wine
- 1 cup parmesan cheese, grated fine & divided
- sea salt & black pepper to taste
- fresh chives, chopped for serving
- lemon wedges for serving

Directions:

Add your broth into a saucepan and bring it to a simmer over medium-high heat. Get out a stock pot and put it over medium-high heat as well. Heat your oil before adding in your onion. Cook for eight minutes and stir occasionally. Add in your barley and cook for two minutes more. Stir in your barley, cooking until it's toasted.

Pour in the wine, cooking for a minute more. Most of the liquid should have evaporated before adding in a cup of warm broth. Cook and stir for two minutes. Your liquid should be absorbed. Add in the remaining broth by the cup, and cook until ach cup is absorbed. It should take about two minutes each time.

Pull out from the heat, add half a cup of cheese, and top with remaining cheese, chives, and lemon wedges.

Nutrition (for 100g): 345 Calories 7g Fat 56g Carbohydrates 14g Protein 912mg Sodium

Seafood & Avocado Salad

Preparation Time : 10 minutes

Cooking Time : 0 minutes

Servings : 4

Difficulty Level : Easy

Ingredients:

- 2 lbs. salmon, cooked & chopped
- 2 lbs. shrimp, cooked & chopped
- 1 cup avocado, chopped
- 1 cup mayonnaise
- 4 tablespoons lime juice, fresh
- 2 cloves garlic
- 1 cup sour cream
- sea salt & black pepper to taste
- ½ red onion, minced
- 1 cup cucumber, chopped

Directions:

Start by getting out a bowl and combine your garlic, salt, pepper, onion, mayonnaise, sour cream and lime juice,

Get out a different bowl and mix together your salmon, shrimp, cucumber, and avocado.

Add the mayonnaise mixture to your shrimp, and then allow it to sit for twenty minutes in the fridge before serving.

Nutrition (for 100g): 394 Calories 30g Fat 3g Carbohydrates 27g Protein 815mg Sodium

Mediterranean Shrimp Salad

Preparation Time : 40 minutes

Cooking Time : 0 minutes

Servings : 6

Difficulty Level : Easy

Ingredients:

- 1 ½ lbs. shrimp, cleaned & cooked
- 2 celery stalks, fresh
- 1 onion
- 2 green onions
- 4 eggs, boiled
- 3 potatoes, cooked
- 3 tablespoons mayonnaise
- sea salt & black pepper to taste

Directions:

Start by slicing your potatoes and chopping your celery. Slice your eggs, and season. Mix everything together. Put your shrimp over the eggs, and then serve with onion and green onions.

Nutrition (for 100g): 207 Calories 6g Fat 15g Carbohydrates 17g Protein 664mg Sodium

Chickpea Pasta Salad

Preparation Time : 10 minutes
Cooking Time : 15 minutes
Servings : 6
Difficulty Level : Average

Ingredients:

- 2 tablespoons olive oil
- 16 ounces rotelle pasta
- ½ cup cured olives, chopped
- 2 tablespoons oregano, fresh & minced
- 2 tablespoons parsley, fresh & chopped
- 1 bunch green onions, chopped
- ¼ cup red wine vinegar
- 15 ounces canned garbanzo beans, drained & rinsed
- ½ cup parmesan cheese, grated
- sea salt & black pepper to taste

Directions:

Boil water and put the pasta al dente and follow per package instructions. Drain it and rinse it using cold water.

Get out a skillet and heat your olive oil over medium heat. Add in your scallions, chickpeas, parsley, oregano and olives. Decrease the heat, and sauté for twenty minutes more. Allow this mixture to cool.

Toss your chickpea mixture with your pasta and add in your grated cheese, salt, pepper and vinegar. Let it chill for four hours or overnight before serving.

Nutrition (for 100g): 424 Calories 10g Fat 69g Carbohydrates 16g Protein 714mg Sodium

Mediterranean Stir Fry

Preparation Time : 10 minutes

Cooking Time : 30 minutes

Servings : 4

Difficulty Level : Average

Ingredients:

- 2 zucchinis
- 1 onion
- ¼ teaspoon sea salt
- 2 cloves garlic
- 3 teaspoons olive oil, divided
- 1 lb. chicken breasts, boneless
- 1 cup quick cooking barley
- 2 cups water
- ¼ teaspoon black pepper
- 1 teaspoon oregano
- ¼ teaspoon red pepper flakes
- ½ teaspoon basil
- 2 plum tomatoes
- ½ cup Greek olives, pitted
- 1 tablespoons parsley, fresh

Directions:

Start by removing the skin from your chicken, and then chop it into smaller pieces. Chop the garlic and parsley, and then chop your olives, zucchini, tomatoes and onions. Get out a saucepan and bring your water to a boil. Mix in your barley, letting it simmer for eight to ten minutes.

Turn off heat. Let it rest for five minutes. Get out a skillet and add in two teaspoons of olive oil. Stir fry your chicken once it's hot, and then remove it from heat. Cook the onion in your remaining oil. Mix in your remaining ingredients, and cook for an additional three to five minutes. Serve warm.

Nutrition (for 100g): 337 Calories 8.6g Fat 32.3g Carbohydrates 31.7g Protein 517mg Sodium

Balsamic Cucumber Salad

Preparation Time : 15 minutes

Cooking Time : 0 minutes

Servings : 4

Difficulty Level : Easy

Ingredients:

- 2/3 large English cucumber, halved and sliced
- 2/3 medium red onion, halved and thinly sliced
- 5 1/2 tablespoons balsamic vinaigrette
- 1 1/3 cups grape tomatoes, halved
- 1/2 cup crumbled reduced-fat feta cheese

Directions:

In a big bowl, mix cucumber, tomatoes and onion. Add vinaigrette; toss to coating. Refrigerate, covered, till serving. Just prior to serving, stir in cheese. Serve with a slotted teaspoon.

Nutrition (for 100g): 250 calories 12g fats 15g carbohydrates 34g protein 633mg Sodium

Beef Kefta Patties with Cucumber Salad

Preparation Time : 10 minutes
Cooking Time : 15 minutes
Servings : 2
Difficulty Level : Difficult

Ingredients:

- cooking spray
- 1/2-pound ground sirloin
- 2 tablespoons plus 2 tablespoons chopped fresh flat-leaf parsley, divided
- 1 1/2 teaspoons chopped peeled fresh ginger
- 1 teaspoon ground coriander
- 2 tablespoons chopped fresh cilantro
- 1/4 teaspoon salt
- 1/2 teaspoon ground cumin
- 1/4 teaspoon ground cinnamon
- 1 cup thinly sliced English cucumbers
- 1 tablespoon rice vinegar
- 1/4 cup plain fat-free Greek yogurt
- 1 1/2 teaspoons fresh lemon juice
- 1/4 teaspoon freshly ground black pepper
- 1 (6-inch) pitas, quartered

Directions:

Warmth a grill skillet over medium-high warmth. Coat pan with cooking spray. Combine beef, 1/4 glass parsley, cilantro, and next 5 elements in a medium bowl. Divide combination into 4 the same portions, shaping each into a 1/2-inch-thick patty. Add patties to pan; cook both sides until desired degree of doneness.

Mix cucumber and vinegar in a medium bowl; throw well. Combine fat-free yogurt, remaining 2 tablespoons parsley, juice, and pepper in a little bowl; stir with a whisk. Set up 1 patty and 1/2 cup cucumber mixture on each of 4 china. Top each offering with about 2 tablespoons yogurt spices. Serve each with 2 pita wedges.

Nutrition (for 100g): 116 calories 5g fats 11g carbohydrates 28g protein 642mg sodium

Chicken and Cucumber Salad with Parsley Pesto

Preparation Time : 15 minutes
Cooking Time : 5 minutes
Servings : 8
Difficulty Level : Easy

Ingredients:

- 2 2/3 cups packed fresh flat-leaf parsley leaves
- 1 1/3 cups fresh baby spinach
- 1 1/2 tablespoons toasted pine nuts
- 1 1/2 tablespoons grated Parmesan cheese
- 2 1/2 tablespoons fresh lemon juice
- 1 1/3 teaspoons kosher salt
- 1/3 teaspoon black pepper
- 1 1/3 medium garlic cloves, smashed
- 2/3 cup extra-virgin olive oil
- 5 1/3 cups shredded rotisserie chicken (from 1 chicken)
- 2 2/3 cups cooked shelled edamame
- 1 1/2 cans 1 (15-oz.) unsalted chickpeas, drained and rinsed
- 1 1/3 cups chopped English cucumbers
- 5 1/3 cups loosely packed arugula

Directions:

Combine parsley, spinach, lemon juice, pine nuts, cheese, garlic, salt, and pepper in food processor; process about 1 minute. With processor running, add oil; process until smooth, about 1 minute.

Stir together chicken, edamame, chickpeas, and cucumber in a large bowl. Add pesto; toss to combine.

Place 2/3 cup arugula in each of 6 bowls; top each with 1 cup chicken salad mixture. Serve immediately.

Nutrition (for 100g): 116 calories 12g fats 3g carbohydrates 9g protein 663mg sodium

Easy Arugula Salad

Preparation Time : 15 minutes
Cooking Time : 0 minutes
Servings : 6
Difficulty Level : Easy

Ingredients:

- 6 cups young arugula leaves, rinsed and dried
- 1 1/2 cups cherry tomatoes, halved
- 6 tablespoons pine nuts
- 3 tablespoons grapeseed oil or olive oil
- 1 1/2 tablespoons rice vinegar
- 3/8 teaspoon freshly ground black pepper to taste
- 6 tablespoons grated Parmesan cheese
- 3/4 teaspoon salt to taste
- 1 1/2 large avocados - peeled, pitted and sliced

Directions:

In a sizable plastic dish with a cover, incorporate arugula, cherry tomatoes, pine nut products, oil, vinegar, and Parmesan cheese. Period with salt and pepper to flavor. Cover, and wring to mix.

Separate salad onto china, and top with slices of avocado.

Nutrition (for 100g): 120 calories 12g fats 14g carbohydrates 25g protein 736mg sodium

Feta Garbanzo Bean Salad

Preparation Time : 10 minutes
Cooking Time : 0 minutes
Servings : 6
Difficulty Level : Easy

Ingredients:

- 1 1/2 cans (15 ounces) garbanzo beans
- 1 1/2 cans (2-1/4 ounces) sliced ripe olives, drained
- 1 1/2 medium tomatoes
- 6 tablespoons thinly sliced red onions
- 2 1/4 cups 1-1/2 coarsely chopped English cucumbers
- 6 tablespoons chopped fresh parsley
- 4 1/2 tablespoons olive oil
- 3/8 teaspoon salt
- 1 1/2 tablespoons lemon juice
- 3/16 teaspoon pepper
- 7 1/2 cups mixed salad greens
- 3/4 cup crumbled feta cheese

Directions:

Transfer all ingredients in a big bowl; toss to combine. Add parmesan cheese.

Nutrition (for 100g): 140 calories 16g fats 10g carbohydrates 24g protein 817mg sodium

Greek Brown and Wild Rice Bowls

Preparation Time : 15 minutes
Cooking Time : 5 minutes
Servings : 4
Difficulty Level : Easy

Ingredients:

- 2 packages (8-1/2 ounces) ready-to-serve whole grain brown and wild rice medley
- 1 medium ripe avocado, peeled and sliced
- 1 1/2 cups cherry tomatoes, halved
- 1/2 cup Greek vinaigrette, divided
- 1/2 cup crumbled feta cheese
- 1/2 cup pitted Greek olives, sliced
- minced fresh parsley, optional

Directions:

Inside a microwave-safe dish, mix the grain mix and 2 tablespoons vinaigrette. Cover and cook on high until warmed through, about 2 minutes. Divide between 2 bowls. Best with avocado, tomato vegetables, cheese, olives, leftover dressing and, if desired, parsley.

Nutrition (for 100g): 116 calories 10g fats 9g carbohydrates 26g protein 607mg sodium

Greek Dinner Salad

Preparation Time : 10 minutes
Cooking Time : 0 minutes
Servings : 4
Difficulty Level : Easy

Ingredients:

- 2 1/2 tablespoons coarsely chopped fresh parsley
- 2 tablespoons coarsely chopped fresh dill
- 2 teaspoons fresh lemon juice
- 2/3 teaspoon dried oregano
- 2 teaspoons extra virgin olive oil
- 4 cups shredded Romaine lettuce
- 2/3 cup thinly sliced red onions
- 1/2 cup crumbled feta cheese
- 2 cups diced tomatoes
- 2 teaspoons capers
- 2/3 cucumber, peeled, quartered lengthwise, and thinly sliced
- 2/3 (19-ounce) can chickpeas, drained and rinsed
- 4 (6-inch) whole wheat pitas, each cut into 8 wedges

Directions:

Combine the first 5 substances in a sizable dish; stir with a whisk. Add a member of the lettuce family and the next 6 ingredients (lettuce through chickpeas); throw well. Serve with pita wedges.

Nutrition (for 100g): 103 calories 12g fats 8g carbohydrates 36g protein 813mg sodium

Halibut with Lemon-Fennel Salad

Preparation Time : 15 minutes
Cooking Time : 5 minutes
Servings : 2
Difficulty Level : Average

Ingredients:

- 1/2 teaspoon ground coriander
- 1/4 teaspoon salt
- 1/8 teaspoon freshly ground black pepper
- 2 1/2 teaspoons extra-virgin olive oils, divided
- 1/4 teaspoon ground cumin
- 1 garlic clove, minced
- 2 (6-ounce) halibut fillets
- 1 cup fennel bulb
- 2 tablespoons thinly vertically sliced red onions
- 1 tablespoon fresh lemon juice
- 1 1/2 teaspoons chopped flat-leaf parsley
- 1/2 teaspoon fresh thyme leaves

Directions:

Combine the first 4 substances in a little dish. Combine 1/2 tsp spice mixture, 2 teaspoons oil, and garlic in a little bowl; rub garlic clove mixture evenly over fish. Heat 1 teaspoon oil in a sizable nonstick frying pan over medium-high high temperature. Add fish to pan; cook 5 minutes on each side or until the desired level of doneness.

Combine remaining 3/4 teaspoon spice mix, remaining 2 tsp oil, fennel light bulb, and remaining substances in a medium bowl, tossing well to coat. Provide salad with seafood.

Nutrition (for 100g): 110 calories 9g fats 11g carbohydrates 29g protein 558mg sodium

Herbed Greek Chicken Salad

Preparation Time : 10 minutes

Cooking Time : 10 minutes

Servings : 2

Difficulty Level : Average

Ingredients:

- 1/2 teaspoon dried oregano
- 1/4 teaspoon garlic powder
- 3/8 teaspoon black pepper, divided
- cooking spray
- 1/2-pound skinless, boneless chicken breasts, cut into 1-inch cubes
- 1/4 teaspoon salt, divided
- 1/2 cup plain fat-free yogurt
- 1 teaspoon tahini (sesame-seed paste)
- 2 1/2 tsps. fresh lemon juice
- 1/2 teaspoon bottled minced garlic
- 4 cups chopped Romaine lettuce
- 1/2 cup peeled chopped English cucumbers
- 1/2 cup grape tomatoes, halved
- 3 pitted kalamata olives, halved
- 2 tablespoons (1 ounce) crumbled feta cheese

Directions:

Combine oregano, garlic natural powder, 1/2 teaspoon pepper, and 1/4 tsp salt in a bowl. Heat a nonstick skillet over medium-high heat. Coating pan with cooking food spray. Add poultry and spice combination; sauté until poultry is done. Drizzle with 1 teaspoon juice; stir. Remove from pan.

Combine remaining 2 teaspoons juice, leftover 1/4 teaspoon sodium, remaining 1/4 tsp pepper, yogurt, tahini, and garlic in a little bowl; mix well. Combine member of the lettuce family, cucumber, tomatoes, and olives. Put 2 1/2 cups of lettuce mixture on each of 4 plates. Top each serving with 1/2 cup chicken combination and 1 teaspoon cheese. Drizzle each serving with 3 tablespoons yogurt combination

Nutrition (for 100g): 116 calories 11g fats 15g carbohydrates 28g protein 634mg sodium

Greek Couscous Salad

Preparation Time : 10 minutes
Cooking Time : 15 minutes
Servings : 10
Difficulty Level : Easy

Ingredients:

- 1 can (14-1/2 ounces) reduced-sodium chicken broth
- 1 1/2 cups 1-3/4 uncooked whole wheat couscous (about 11 ounces)
- Dressing:
- 6 1/2 tablespoons olive oil
- 1 1/4 teaspoons 1-1/2 grated lemon zest
- 3 1/2 tablespoons lemon juice
- 13/16 teaspoon adobo seasonings
- 3/16 teaspoon salt
- Salad:
- 1 2/3 cups grape tomatoes, halved
- 5/6 English cucumber, halved lengthwise and sliced
- 3/4 cup coarsely chopped fresh parsley
- 1 can (6-1/2 ounces) sliced ripe olives, drained
- 6 1/2 tablespoons crumbled feta cheese
- 3 1/3 green onions, chopped

Directions:

In a sizable saucepan, bring broth to a boil. Stir in couscous. Remove from heat; let stand, covered, until broth is absorbed, about 5 minutes. Transfer to a sizable dish; cool completely.

Beat together dressing substances. Add cucumber, tomato vegetables, parsley, olives and green onions to couscous; stir in dressing. Gently mix in cheese. Provide immediately or refrigerate and serve frosty.

Nutrition (for 100g): 114 calories 13g fats 18g carbohydrates 27g protein 811mg sodium

Denver Fried Omelet

Preparation Time : 10 minutes

Cooking Time : 30 minutes

Servings : 4

Difficulty Level : Average

Ingredients:

- 2 tablespoons butter
- 1/2 onion, minced meat
- 1/2 green pepper, minced
- 1 cup chopped cooked ham
- 8 eggs
- 1/4 cup of milk
- 1/2 cup grated cheddar cheese and ground black pepper to taste

Directions:

Preheat the oven to 200 degrees C (400 degrees F). Grease a round baking dish of 10 inches.

Melt the butter over medium heat; cook and stir onion and pepper until soft, about 5 minutes. Stir in the ham and keep cooking until everything is hot for 5 minutes.

Whip the eggs and milk in a large bowl. Stir in the mixture of cheddar cheese and ham; Season with salt and black pepper. Pour the mixture in a baking dish. Bake in the oven, about 25 minutes. Serve hot.

Nutrition (for 100g): 345 Calories 26.8g Fat 3.6g Carbohydrates 22.4g Protein 712 mg Sodium

Sausage Pan

Preparation Time : 25 minutes

Cooking Time : 60 minutes

Servings : 12

Difficulty Level : Average

Ingredients:

- 1-pound Sage Breakfast Sausage,
- 3 cups grated potatoes, drained and squeezed
- 1/4 cup melted butter,
- 12 oz soft grated Cheddar cheese
- 1/2 cup onion, grated
- 1 (16 oz) small cottage cheese container
- 6 giant eggs

Directions:

Set up the oven to 190 ° C. Grease a 9 x 13-inch square oven dish lightly.

Place the sausage in a big deep-frying pan. Bake over medium heat until smooth. Drain, crumble, and reserve.

Mix the grated potatoes and butter in the prepared baking dish. Cover the bottom and sides of the dish with the mixture. Combine in a bowl sausage, cheddar, onion, cottage cheese, and eggs. Pour over the potato mixture. Let it bake.

Allow cooling for 5 minutes before serving.

Nutrition (for 100g): 355 Calories 26.3g Fat 7.9g Carbohydrates 21.6g Protein 755mg Sodium.

Grilled Marinated Shrimp

Preparation Time : 30 minutes
Cooking Time : 60 minutes
Servings : 6
Difficulty Level : Easy

Ingredients:

- 1 cup olive oil,
- 1/4 cup chopped fresh parsley
- 1 lemon, juiced,
- 3 cloves of garlic, finely chopped
- 1 tablespoon tomato puree
- 2 teaspoons dried oregano,
- 1 teaspoon salt
- 2 tablespoons hot pepper sauce
- 1 teaspoon ground black pepper,
- 2 pounds of shrimp, peeled and stripped of tails

Directions:

Combine olive oil, parsley, lemon juice, hot sauce, garlic, tomato puree, oregano, salt, and black pepper in a bowl. Reserve a small amount to string later. Fill the large, resealable plastic bag with marinade and shrimp. Close and let it chill for 2 hours.

Preheat the grill on medium heat. Thread shrimp on skewers, poke once at the tail, and once at the head. Discard the marinade.

Lightly oil the grill. Cook the prawns for 5 minutes on each side or until they are opaque, often baste with the reserved marinade.

Nutrition (for 100g): 447 Calories 37.5g Fat 3.7g Carbohydrates 25.3g Protein 800mg Sodium

Sausage Egg Casserole

Preparation Time : 20 minutes

Cooking Time : 1 hour 10 minutes

Servings : 12

Difficulty Level : Average

Ingredients:

- 3/4-pound finely chopped pork sausage
- 1 tablespoon butter
- 4 green onions, minced meat
- 1/2 pound of fresh mushrooms
- 10 eggs, beaten
- 1 container (16 grams) low-fat cottage cheese
- 1 pound of Monterey Jack Cheese, grated
- 2 cans of a green pepper diced, drained
- 1 cup flour, 1 teaspoon baking powder
- 1/2 teaspoon salt
- 1/3 cup melted butter

Directions:

Put sausage in a deep-frying pan. Bake over medium heat until smooth. Drain and set aside. Melt the butter in a pan, cook and stir the green onions and mushrooms until they are soft.

Combine eggs, cottage cheese, Monterey Jack cheese, and peppers in a large bowl. Stir in sausages, green onions, and mushrooms. Cover and spend the night in the fridge.

Setup the oven to 175 ° C (350 ° F). Grease a 9 x 13-inch light baking dish.

Sift the flour, baking powder, and salt into a bowl. Stir in the melted butter. Incorporate flour mixture into the egg mixture. Pour into the prepared baking dish. Bake until lightly browned. Let stand for 10 minutes before serving.

Nutrition (for 100g): 408 Calories 28.7g Fat 12.4g Carbohydrates 25.2g Protein 1095mg Sodium

Baked Omelet Squares

Preparation Time : 15 minutes
Cooking Time : 30 minutes
Servings : 8
Difficulty Level : Easy

Ingredients:

- 1/4 cup butter
- 1 small onion, minced meat
- 1 1/2 cups grated cheddar cheese
- 1 can of sliced mushrooms
- 1 can slice black olives cooked ham (optional)
- sliced jalapeno peppers (optional)
- 12 eggs, scrambled eggs
- 1/2 cup of milk
- salt and pepper, to taste

Directions:

Prepare the oven to 205 ° C (400 ° F). Grease a 9 x 13-inch baking dish.

Cook the butter in a frying pan over medium heat and cook the onion until done.

Lay out the Cheddar cheese on the bottom of the prepared baking dish. Layer with mushrooms, olives, fried onion, ham, and jalapeno peppers. Stir the eggs in a bowl with milk, salt, and pepper. Pour the egg mixture over the ingredients, but do not mix.

Bake in the uncovered and preheated oven, until no more liquid flows in the middle and is light brown above. Allow to cool a little, then cut it into squares and serve.

Nutrition (for 100g): 344 Calories 27.3g Fat 7.2g Carbohydrates 17.9g Protein 1087mg Sodium

Hard-Boiled Egg

Preparation Time : 5 minutes
Cooking Time : 15 minutes
Servings : 8
Difficulty Level : Easy

Ingredients:

- 1 tablespoon of salt
- 1/4 cup distilled white vinegar
- 6 cups of water
- 8 eggs

Directions:

Place the salt, vinegar, and water in a large saucepan and bring to a boil over high heat. Stir in the eggs one by one, and be careful not to split them. Lower the heat and cook over low heat and cook for 14 minutes.

Pull out the eggs from the hot water and place them in a container filled with ice water or cold water. Cool completely, approximately 15 minutes.

Nutrition (for 100g): 72 Calories 5g Fat 0.4g Carbohydrates 6.3g Protein 947 mg Sodium

Mushrooms with a Soy Sauce Glaze

Preparation Time : 5 minutes

Cooking Time : 10 minutes

Servings : 2

Difficulty Level : Average

Ingredients:

- 2 tablespoons butter
- 1(8 ounces) package sliced white mushrooms
- 2 cloves garlic, minced
- 2 teaspoons soy sauce
- ground black pepper to taste

Directions:

Cook the butter in a frying pan over medium heat; stir in the mushrooms; cook and stir until the mushrooms are soft and released about 5 minutes. Stir in the garlic; keep cooking and stir for 1 minute. Pour the soy sauce; cook the mushrooms in the soy sauce until the liquid has evaporated, about 4 minutes.

Nutrition (for 100g): 135 Calories 11.9g Fat 5.4g Carbohydrates

Pepperoni Eggs

Preparation Time : 10 minutes

Cooking Time : 20 minutes

Servings : 2

Difficulty Level : Average

Ingredients:

- 1 cup of egg substitute
- 1 egg
- 3 green onions, minced meat
- 8 slices of pepperoni, diced
- 1/2 teaspoon of garlic powder
- 1 teaspoon melted butter
- 1/4 cup grated Romano cheese
- salt and ground black pepper to taste

Directions:

Combine the egg substitute, the egg, the green onions, the pepperoni slices, and the garlic powder in a bowl.

Cook the butter in a non-stick frying pan over low heat; Add the egg mixture, seal the pan and cook 10 to 15 minutes. Sprinkle Romano's eggs and season with salt and pepper.

Nutrition (for 100g): 266 Calories 16.2g Fat 3.7g Carbohydrates 25.3g Protein 586mg Sodium

Egg Cupcakes

Preparation Time : 15 minutes
Cooking Time : 20 minutes
Servings : 6
Difficulty Level : Average

Ingredients:

- 1 pack of bacon (12 ounces)
- 6 eggs
- 2 tablespoons of milk
- 1/4 teaspoon salt
- 1/4 teaspoon ground black pepper
- 1 c. Melted butter
- 1/4 teaspoon. Dried parsley
- 1/2 cup ham
- 1/4 cup mozzarella cheese
- 6 slices gouda

Directions:

Prepare the oven to 175 ° C (350 ° F). Cook bacon over medium heat, until it starts to brown. Dry the bacon slices with kitchen paper.

Situate the slices of bacon in the 6 cups of the non-stick muffin pan. Slice the remaining bacon and put it at the bottom of each cup.

Mix eggs, milk, butter, parsley, salt, and pepper. Add in the ham and mozzarella cheese.

Fill the cups with the egg mixture; garnish with Gouda cheese.

Bake in the preheated oven until Gouda cheese is melted and the eggs are tender about 15 minutes.

Nutrition (for 100g): 310 Calories 22.9g Fat 2.1g Carbohydrates 23.1g Protein 988mg Sodium.

Dinosaur Eggs

Preparation Time : 20 minutes
Cooking Time : 15 minutes
Servings : 4
Difficulty Level : Difficult

Ingredients:

- Mustard sauce:
- 1/4 cup coarse mustard
- 1/4 cup Greek yogurt
- 1 teaspoon garlic powder
- 1 pinch of cayenne pepper
- Eggs:
- 2 beaten eggs
- 2 cups of mashed potato flakes
- 4 boiled eggs, peeled
- 1 can (15 oz) HORMEL® Mary Kitchen® minced beef finely chopped can
- 2 liters of vegetable oil for frying

Directions:

Combine the old-fashioned mustard, Greek yogurt, garlic powder, and cayenne pepper in a small bowl until smooth.

Transfer the 2 beaten eggs in a shallow dish; place the potato flakes in a separate shallow dish.

Divide the minced meat into 4 Servings. Form salted beef around each egg until it is completely wrapped.

Soak the wrapped eggs in the beaten egg and brush with mashed potatoes until they are covered.

Fill the oil in a large saucepan and heat at 190 ° C (375 ° F).

Put 2 eggs in the hot oil and bake for 3 to 5 minutes until brown. Remove with a drop of spoon and place on a plate lined with kitchen paper. Repeat this with the remaining 2 eggs.

Cut lengthwise and serve with a mustard sauce.

Nutrition (for 100g): 784 Calories 63.2g Fat 34g Carbohydrates

Dill and Tomato Frittata

Preparation Time : 10 minutes

Cooking Time : 35 minutes

Servings : 6

Difficulty Level : Average

Ingredients:

- Pepper and salt to taste
- 1 teaspoon red pepper flakes
- 2 garlic cloves, minced
- ½ cup crumbled goat cheese – optional
- 2 tablespoon fresh chives, chopped
- 2 tablespoon fresh dill, chopped
- 4 tomatoes, diced
- 8 eggs, whisked
- 1 teaspoon coconut oil

Directions:

Grease a 9-inch round baking pan and preheat oven to 325oF.

In a large bowl, mix well all ingredients and pour into prepped pan.

Lay into the oven and bake until middle is cooked through around 30-35 minutes.

Remove from oven and garnish with more chives and dill.

Nutrition (for 100g): 149 Calories 10.28g Fat 9.93g Carbohydrates 13.26g Protein 523mg Sodium

Paleo Almond Banana Pancakes

Preparation Time : 10 minutes
Cooking Time : 10 minutes
Servings : 3
Difficulty Level : Average

Ingredients:

- ¼ cup almond flour
- ½ teaspoon ground cinnamon
- 3 eggs
- 1 banana, mashed
- 1 tablespoon almond butter
- 1 teaspoon vanilla extract
- 1 teaspoon olive oil
- Sliced banana to serve

Directions:

Whip eggs in a bowl until fluffy. In another bowl, mash the banana using a fork and add to the egg mixture. Add the vanilla, almond butter, cinnamon and almond flour. Mix into a smooth batter. Heat the olive oil in a skillet. Add one spoonful of the batter and fry them on both sides.

Keep doing these steps until you are done with all the batter.

Add some sliced banana on top before serving.

Nutrition (for 100g): 306 Calories 26g Fat 3.6g Carbohydrates 14.4g Protein 588mg Sodium

Zucchini with Egg

Preparation Time : 5 minutes
Cooking Time : 10 minutes
Servings : 2
Difficulty Level : Easy

Ingredients:

- 1 1/2 tablespoons olive oil
- 2 large zucchinis, cut into large chunks
- salt and ground black pepper to taste
- 2 large eggs
- 1 teaspoon water, or as desired

Directions:

Cook the oil in a frying pan over medium heat; sauté zucchini until soft, about 10 minutes. Season the zucchini well.

Lash the eggs using a fork in a bowl. Pour in water and beat until everything is well mixed. Pour the eggs over the zucchini; boil and stir until scrambled eggs and no more flowing, about 5 minutes. Season well the zucchini and eggs.

Nutrition (for 100g): 213 Calories 15.7g Fat 11.2g Carbohydrates 10.2g Protein 180mg Sodium

Cheesy Amish Breakfast Casserole

Preparation Time : 10 minutes
Cooking Time : 50 minutes
Servings : 12
Difficulty Level : Easy

Ingredients:

- 1-pound sliced bacon, diced,
- 1 sweet onion, minced meat
- 4 cups grated and frozen potatoes, thawed
- 9 lightly beaten eggs
- 2 cups of grated cheddar cheese
- 1 1/2 cup of cottage cheese
- 1 1/4 cups of grated Swiss cheese

Directions:

Preheat the oven to 175 ° C (350 ° F). Grease a 9 x 13-inch baking dish.

Warm up large frying pan over medium heat; cook and stir the bacon and onion until the bacon is evenly browned about 10 minutes. Drain. Stir in potatoes, eggs, cheddar cheese, cottage cheese, and Swiss cheese. Fill the mixture into a prepared baking dish.

Bake in the oven until the eggs are cooked and the cheese is melted 45 to 50 minutes. Set aside for 10 minutes before cutting and serving.

Nutrition (for 100g): 314 Calories 22.8g Fat 12.1g Carbohydrates 21.7g Protein 609mg Sodium

Salad with Roquefort Cheese

Preparation Time : 20 minutes

Cooking Time : 25 minutes

Servings : 6

Difficulty Level : Easy

Ingredients:

- 1 leaf lettuce, torn into bite-sized pieces
- 3 pears - peeled, without a core and cut into pieces
- 5 oz Roquefort cheese, crumbled
- 1/2 cup chopped green onions
- 1 avocado - peeled, seeded and diced
- 1/4 cup white sugar
- 1/2 cup pecan nuts
- 1 1/2 teaspoon white sugar
- 1/3 cup olive oil,
- 3 tablespoons red wine vinegar,
- 1 1/2 teaspoons prepared mustard,
- 1 clove of chopped garlic,
- 1/2 teaspoon ground fresh black pepper

Directions:

Incorporate 1/4 cup of sugar with the pecans in a frying pan over medium heat. Continue to stir gently until the sugar has melted with pecans. Carefully situate the nuts to wax paper. Set aside and break into pieces.

Combination for vinaigrette oil, vinegar, 1 1/2 teaspoon of sugar, mustard, chopped garlic, salt, and pepper.

In a large bowl, mix lettuce, pears, blue cheese, avocado, and green onions. Pour vinaigrette over salad, topped with pecans and serve.

Nutrition (for 100g): 426 Calories 31.6g Fat 33.1g Carbohydrates 8g Protein 654mg Sodium

Rice with Vermicelli

Preparation Time : 5 minutes

Cooking Time : 45 minutes

Servings : 6

Difficulty Level : Easy

Ingredients:

- 2 cups short-grain rice
- 3½ cups water, plus more for rinsing and soaking the rice
- ¼ cup olive oil
- 1 cup broken vermicelli pasta
- Salt

Directions:

Soak the rice under cold water until the water runs clean. Place the rice in a bowl, cover with water, and let soak for 10 minutes. Drain and set aside. Cook the olive oil in a medium pot over medium heat.

Stir in the vermicelli and cook for 2 to 3 minutes, stirring continuously, until golden.

Put the rice and cook for 1 minute, stirring, so the rice is well coated in the oil. Stir in the water and a pinch of salt and bring the liquid to a boil. Adjust heat and simmer for 20 minutes. Pull out from the heat and let rest for 10 minutes. Fluff with a fork and serve.

Nutrition (for 100g): 346 calories 9g total fat 60g carbohydrates 2g protein 0.9mg sodium

Fava Beans and Rice

Preparation Time : 10 minutes

Cooking Time : 35 minutes

Servings : 4

Difficulty Level : Easy

Ingredients:

- ¼ cup olive oil
- 4 cups fresh fava beans, shelled
- 4½ cups water, plus more for drizzling
- 2 cups basmati rice
- 1/8 teaspoon salt
- 1/8 teaspoon freshly ground black pepper
- 2 tablespoons pine nuts, toasted
- ½ cup chopped fresh garlic chives, or fresh onion chives

Directions:

Fill the sauce pan with olive oil and cook over medium heat. Add the fava beans and drizzle them with a bit of water to avoid burning or sticking. Cook for 10 minutes.

Gently stir in the rice. Add the water, salt, and pepper. Set up the heat and boil the mixture. Adjust the heat and let it simmer for 15 minutes.

Pull out from the heat and let it rest for 10 minutes before serving. Spoon onto a serving platter and sprinkle with the toasted pine nuts and chives.

Nutrition (for 100g): 587 calories 17g total fat 97g carbohydrates 2g protein 0.6mg sodium

Buttered Fava Beans

Preparation Time : 30 minutes
Cooking Time : 15 minutes
Servings : 4
Difficulty Level : Easy

Ingredients:

- ½ cup vegetable broth
- 4 pounds fava beans, shelled
- ¼ cup fresh tarragon, divided
- 1 teaspoon chopped fresh thyme
- ¼ teaspoon freshly ground black pepper
- 1/8 teaspoon salt
- 2 tablespoons butter
- 1 garlic clove, minced
- 2 tablespoons chopped fresh parsley

Directions:

Boil vegetable broth in a shallow pan over medium heat. Add the fava beans, 2 tablespoons of tarragon, the thyme, pepper, and salt. Cook until the broth is almost absorbed and the beans are tender.

Stir in the butter, garlic, and remaining 2 tablespoons of tarragon. Cook for 2 to 3 minutes. Sprinkle with the parsley and serve hot.

Nutrition (for 100g): 458 calories 9g fat 81g carbohydrates 37g protein 691mg sodium

Freekeh

Preparation Time : 10 minutes
Cooking Time : 40 minutes
Servings : 4
Difficulty Level : Easy

Ingredients:

- 4 tablespoons Ghee
- 1 onion, chopped
- 3½ cups vegetable broth
- 1 teaspoon ground allspice
- 2 cups freekeh
- 2 tablespoons pine nuts, toasted

Directions:

Melt ghee in a heavy-bottomed saucepan over medium heat. Stir in the onion and cook for about 5 minutes, stirring constantly, until the onion is golden. Pour in the vegetable broth, add the allspice, and bring to a boil. Stir in the freekeh and return the mixture to a boil. Adjust heat and simmer for 30 minutes, stir occasionally. Spoon the freekeh into a serving dish and top with the toasted pine nuts.

Nutrition (for 100g): 459 calories 18g fat 64g carbohydrates 10g protein 692mg sodium

Fried Rice Balls with Tomato Sauce

Preparation Time : 15 minutes
Cooking Time : 20 minutes
Servings : 8
Difficulty Level : Difficult

Ingredients:

- 1 cup bread crumbs
- 2 cups cooked risotto
- 2 large eggs, divided
- ¼ cup freshly grated Parmesan cheese
- 8 fresh baby mozzarella balls, or 1 (4-inch) log fresh mozzarella, cut into 8 pieces
- 2 tablespoons water
- 1 cup corn oil
- 1 cup Basic Tomato Basil Sauce, or store-bought

Directions:

Situate the bread crumbs into a small bowl and set aside. In a medium bowl, stir together the risotto, 1 egg, and the Parmesan cheese until well. Split the risotto mixture into 8 pieces. Situate them on a clean work surface and flatten each piece.

Place 1 mozzarella ball on each flattened rice disk. Close the rice around the mozzarella to form a ball. Repeat until you finish all the balls. In the same medium, now-empty bowl, whisk the remaining egg and the water. Dip each prepared risotto ball into the egg wash and roll it in the bread crumbs. Set aside.

Cook corn oil in a skillet over high heat. Gently lower the risotto balls into the hot oil and fry for 5 to 8 minutes until golden brown. Stir them, as needed, to ensure the entire surface is fried. Using a slotted spoon, put the fried balls to paper towels to drain.

Warm up the tomato sauce in a medium saucepan over medium heat for 5 minutes, stir occasionally, and serve the warm sauce alongside the rice balls.

Nutrition (for 100g): 255 calories 15g fat 16g carbohydrates 2g protein 669mg sodium

Spanish-Style Rice

Preparation Time : 10 minutes

Cooking Time : 35 minutes

Servings : 4

Difficulty Level : Average

Ingredients:

- ¼ cup olive oil
- 1 small onion, finely chopped
- 1 red bell pepper, seeded and diced
- 1½ cups white rice
- 1 teaspoon sweet paprika
- ½ teaspoon ground cumin
- ½ teaspoon ground coriander
- 1 garlic clove, minced
- 3 tablespoons tomato paste
- 3 cups vegetable broth
- 1/8 teaspoon salt

Directions:

Cook the olive oil in a large heavy-bottomed skillet over medium heat. Stir in the onion and red bell pepper. Cook for 5 minutes or until softened. Add the rice, paprika, cumin, and coriander and cook for 2 minutes, stirring often.

Add the garlic, tomato paste, vegetable broth, and salt. Stir it well and season, as needed. Allow the mixture to a boil. Lower heat and simmer for 20 minutes.

Set aside for 5 minutes before serving.

Nutrition (for 100g): 414 calories 14g fat 63g carbohydrates 2g protein 664mg sodium

Zucchini with Rice and Tzatziki

Preparation Time : 20 minutes
Cooking Time : 35 minutes
Servings : 4
Difficulty Level : Average

Ingredients:

- ¼ cup olive oil
- 1 onion, chopped
- 3 zucchinis, diced
- 1 cup vegetable broth
- ½ cup chopped fresh dill
- Salt
- Freshly ground black pepper
- 1 cup short-grain rice
- 2 tablespoons pine nuts
- 1 cup Tzatziki Sauce, Plain Yogurt, or store-bought

Directions:

Cook oil in a heavy-bottomed pot over medium heat. Stir in the onion, turn the heat to medium-low, and sauté for 5 minutes. Mix in the zucchini and cook for 2 minutes more.

Stir in the vegetable broth and dill and season with salt and pepper. Turn up heat to medium and bring the mixture to a boil.

Stir in the rice and place the mixture back to a boil. Set the heat to very low, cover the pot, and cook for 15 minutes. Pull out from the heat and set aside, for 10 minutes. Scoop the rice onto a serving platter, sprinkle with the pine nuts, and serve with tzatziki sauce.

Nutrition (for 100g): 414 calories 17g fat 57g carbohydrates 5g protein 591mg sodium

Cannellini Beans with Rosemary and Garlic Aioli

Preparation Time : 10 minutes
Cooking Time : 10 minutes
Servings : 4
Difficulty Level : Easy

Ingredients:

- 4 cups cooked cannellini beans
- 4 cups water
- ½ teaspoon salt
- 3 tablespoons olive oil
- 2 tablespoons chopped fresh rosemary
- ½ cup Garlic Aioli
- ¼ teaspoon freshly ground black pepper

Directions:

Mix the cannellini beans, water, and salt in a medium saucepan over medium heat. Bring to a boil. Cook for 5 minutes. Drain. Cook the olive oil in a skillet over medium heat.

Add the beans. Stir in the rosemary and aioli. Adjust heat to medium-low and cook, stirring, just to heat through. Season with pepper and serve.

Nutrition (for 100g): 545 calories 36g fat 42g carbohydrates 14g protein 608mg sodium

Jeweled Rice

Preparation Time : 15 minutes
Cooking Time : 30 minutes
Servings : 6
Difficulty Level : Difficult

Ingredients:

- ½ cup olive oil, divided
- 1 onion, finely chopped
- 1 garlic clove, minced
- ½ teaspoon chopped peeled fresh ginger
- 4½ cups water
- 1 teaspoon salt, divided, plus more as needed
- 1 teaspoon ground turmeric
- 2 cups basmati rice
- 1 cup fresh sweet peas
- 2 carrots, peeled and cut into ½-inch dice
- ½ cup dried cranberries
- Grated zest of 1 orange
- 1/8 teaspoon cayenne pepper
- ¼ cup slivered almonds, toasted

Directions:

Warm up ¼ cup of olive oil in a large pan. Place the onion and cook for 4 minutes. Sauté in the garlic and ginger.

Stir in the water, ¾ teaspoon of salt, and the turmeric. Bring the mixture to a boil. Put in the rice and return the mixture to a boil. Taste the broth and season with more salt, as needed. Select the heat to low, and cook for 15 minutes. Turn off the heat. Let the rice rest on the burner, covered, for 10 minutes. Meanwhile, in a medium sauté pan or skillet over medium-low heat, heat the remaining ¼ cup of olive oil. Stir in the peas and carrots. Cook for 5 minutes.

Stir in the cranberries and orange zest. Dust with the remaining salt and the cayenne. Cook for 1 to 2 minutes. Spoon the rice onto a serving platter. Top with the peas and carrots and sprinkle with the toasted almonds.

Nutrition (for 100g): 460 calories 19g fat 65g carbohydrates 4g protein 810mg sodium

Asparagus Risotto

Preparation Time : 15 minutes
Cooking Time : 30 minutes
Servings : 4
Difficulty Level : Difficult

Ingredients:

- 5 cups vegetable broth, divided
- 3 tablespoons unsalted butter, divided
- 1 tablespoon olive oil
- 1 small onion, chopped
- 1½ cups Arborio rice
- 1-pound fresh asparagus, ends trimmed, cut into 1-inch pieces, tips separated
- ¼ cup freshly grated Parmesan cheese

Directions:

Boil the vegetable broth over medium heat. Set the heat to low and simmer. Mix 2 tablespoons of butter with the olive oil. Stir in the onion and cook for 2 to 3 minutes.

Put the rice and stir with a wooden spoon while cooking for 1 minute until the grains are well covered with butter and oil.

Stir in ½ cup of warm broth. Cook and continue stirring until the broth is completely absorbed. Add the asparagus stalks and another ½ cup of broth. Cook and stir occasionally Continue adding the broth, ½ cup at a time, and cooking until it is completely absorbed upon adding the next ½ cup. Stir frequently to prevent sticking. Rice should be cooked but still firm.

Add the asparagus tips, the remaining 1 tablespoon of butter, and the Parmesan cheese. Stir vigorously to combine. Remove from the heat, top with additional Parmesan cheese, if desired, and serve immediately.

Nutrition (for 100g): 434 calories 14g fat 67g carbohydrates 6g protein 517mg sodium

Moroccan Tagine with Vegetables

Preparation Time : 20 minutes

Cooking Time : 40 minutes

Servings : 2

Difficulty Level : Average

Ingredients:

- 2 tablespoons olive oil
- ½ onion, diced
- 1 garlic clove, minced
- 2 cups cauliflower florets
- 1 medium carrot, cut into 1-inch pieces
- 1 cup diced eggplant
- 1 can whole tomatoes with juices
- 1 (15-ounce / 425-g) can chickpeas
- 2 small red potatoes
- 1 cup water
- 1 teaspoon pure maple syrup
- ½ teaspoon cinnamon
- ½ teaspoon turmeric
- 1 teaspoon cumin
- ½ teaspoon salt
- 1 to 2 teaspoons harissa paste

Directions:

In a Dutch oven, heat up the olive oil over medium-high heat. Sauté the onion for 5 minutes, stirring occasionally, or until the onion is translucent.

Stir in the garlic, cauliflower florets, carrot, eggplant, tomatoes, and potatoes. Mash tomatoes by using a wooden spoon into smaller pieces.

Add the chickpeas, water, maple syrup, cinnamon, turmeric, cumin, and salt and stir to incorporate. Let it boil

Once done, reduce the heat to medium-low. Stir in the harissa paste, cover, allow to simmer for about 40 minutes, or until the vegetables are softened. Taste and adjust seasoning as needed. Let it rest before serving.

Nutrition (for 100g): 293 Calories 9.9g Fat 12.1g Carbohydrates 11.2g Protein 811mg Sodium

Chickpea Lettuce Wraps with Celery

Preparation Time : 10 minutes

Cooking Time : 0 minutes

Servings : 4

Difficulty Level : Easy

Ingredients:

- 1 (15-ounce / 425-g) can low-sodium chickpeas
- 1 celery stalk, thinly sliced
- 2 tablespoons finely chopped red onion
- 2 tablespoons unsalted tahini
- 3 tablespoons honey mustard
- 1 tablespoon capers, undrained
- 12 butter lettuce leaves

Directions:

In a bowl, puree the chickpeas with a potato masher or the back of a fork until mostly smooth. Add the celery, red onion, tahini, honey mustard, and capers to the bowl and stir until well incorporated.

For each serving, place three overlapping lettuce leaves on a plate and top with ¼ of the mashed chickpea filling, then roll up. Repeat with the remaining lettuce leaves and chickpea mixture.

Nutrition (for 100g): 182 Calories 7.1g Fat 3g Carbohydrates 10.3g Protein 743mg Sodium

Grilled Vegetable Skewers

Preparation Time : 15 minutes

Cooking Time : 10 minutes

Servings : 4

Difficulty Level : Easy

Ingredients:

- 4 medium red onions, peeled and sliced into 6 wedges
- 4 medium zucchinis, cut into 1-inch-thick slices
- 2 beefsteak tomatoes, cut into quarters
- 4 red bell peppers
- 2 orange bell peppers
- 2 yellow bell peppers
- 2 tablespoons plus 1 teaspoon olive oil

Directions:

Preheat the grill to medium-high heat. Skewer the vegetables by alternating between red onion, zucchini, tomatoes, and the different colored bell peppers. Grease them with 2 tablespoons of olive oil.

Oil the grill grates with 1 teaspoon of olive oil and grill the vegetable skewers for 5 minutes. Flip the skewers and grill for 5 minutes more, or until they are cooked to your liking. Let the skewers cool for 5 minutes before serving.

Nutrition (for 100g): 115 Calories 3g Fat 4.7g Carbohydrates 3.5g Protein 647mg Sodium

Stuffed Portobello Mushroom with Tomatoes

Preparation Time : 10 minutes
Cooking Time : 15 minutes
Servings : 4
Difficulty Level : Average

Ingredients:

- 4 large portobello mushroom caps
- 3 tablespoons extra-virgin olive oil
- Salt and black pepper, to taste
- 4 sun-dried tomatoes
- 1 cup shredded mozzarella cheese, divided
- ½ to ¾ cup low-sodium tomato sauce

Directions:

Preheat the broiler on high. Lay the mushroom caps on a baking sheet and drizzle with olive oil. Sprinkle with salt and pepper. Broil for 1o minutes, flipping the mushroom caps halfway through, until browned on the top.

Remove from the broil. Spoon 1 tomato, 2 tablespoons of cheese, and 2 to 3 tablespoons of sauce onto each mushroom cap. Return the mushroom caps to the broiler and continue broiling for 2 to 3 minutes. Cool for 5 minutes before serving.

Nutrition (for 100g): 217 Calories 15.8g Fat 9g Carbohydrates 11.2g Protein 793mg Sodium

Wilted Dandelion Greens with Sweet Onion

Preparation Time : 15 minutes
Cooking Time : 15 minutes
Servings : 4
Difficulty Level : Easy

Ingredients:

- 1 tablespoon extra-virgin olive oil
- 2 garlic cloves, minced
- 1 Vidalia onion, thinly sliced
- ½ cup low-sodium vegetable broth
- 2 bunches dandelion greens, roughly chopped
- Freshly ground black pepper, to taste

Directions:

Heat up the olive oil in a large skillet over low heat. Add the garlic and onion and cook for 2 to 3 minutes, stirring occasionally, or until the onion is translucent.

Fold in the vegetable broth and dandelion greens and cook for 5 to 7 minutes until wilted, stirring frequently. Sprinkle with the black pepper and serve on a plate while warm.

Nutrition (for 100g): 81 Calories 3.9g Fat 4g Carbohydrates 3.2g Protein 693mg Sodium

Celery and Mustard Greens

Preparation Time : 10 minutes

Cooking Time : 15 minutes

Servings : 4

Difficulty Level : Average

Ingredients:

- ½ cup low-sodium vegetable broth
- 1 celery stalk, roughly chopped
- ½ sweet onion, chopped
- ½ large red bell pepper, thinly sliced
- 2 garlic cloves, minced
- 1 bunch mustard greens, roughly chopped

Directions:

Pour the vegetable broth into a large cast iron pan and bring it to a simmer over medium heat. Stir in the celery, onion, bell pepper, and garlic. Cook uncovered for about 3 to 5 minutes.

Add the mustard greens to the pan and stir well. Decrease heat and cook until the liquid is evaporated and the greens are wilted. Remove from the heat and serve warm.

Nutrition (for 100g): 39 Calories 3.1g Protein 6.8g Carbohydrates 3g Protein 736mg Sodium

Vegetable and Tofu Scramble

Preparation Time : 5 minutes

Cooking Time : 10 minutes

Servings : 2

Difficulty Level : Easy

Ingredients:

- 2 tablespoons extra-virgin olive oil
- ½ red onion, finely chopped
- 1 cup chopped kale
- 8 ounces (227 g) mushrooms, sliced
- 8 ounces (227 g) tofu, cut into pieces
- 2 garlic cloves, minced
- Pinch red pepper flakes
- ½ teaspoon sea salt
- 1/8 teaspoon freshly ground black pepper

Directions:

Cook the olive oil in a medium nonstick skillet over medium-high heat until shimmering. Add the onion, kale, and mushrooms to the skillet. Cook and stirring irregularly, or until the vegetables start to brown.

Add the tofu and stir-fry for 3 to 4 minutes until softened. Stir in the garlic, red pepper flakes, salt, and black pepper and cook for 30 seconds. Let it rest before serving.

Nutrition (for 100g): 233 Calories 15.9g Fat 2g Carbohydrates 13.4g Protein 733mg Sodium

Simple Zoodles

Preparation Time : 10 minutes
Cooking Time : 5 minutes
Servings : 2
Difficulty Level : Easy

Ingredients:

- 2 tablespoons avocado oil
- 2 medium zucchinis, spiralized
- ¼ teaspoon salt
- Freshly ground black pepper, to taste

Directions:

Warm up the avocado oil in a large skillet over medium heat until it shimmers. Add the zucchini noodles, salt, and black pepper to the skillet and toss to coat. Cook and stir continuously, until tender. Serve warm.

Nutrition (for 100g): 128 Calories 14g Fat 0.3g Carbohydrates 0.3g Protein 811mg Sodium

Lentil and Tomato Collard Wraps

Preparation Time : 15 minutes

Cooking Time : 0 minutes

Servings : 4

Difficulty Level : Easy

Ingredients:

- 2 cups cooked lentils
- 5 Roma tomatoes, diced
- ½ cup crumbled feta cheese
- 10 large fresh basil leaves, thinly sliced
- ¼ cup extra-virgin olive oil
- 1 tablespoon balsamic vinegar
- 2 garlic cloves, minced
- ½ teaspoon raw honey
- ½ teaspoon salt
- ¼ teaspoon freshly ground black pepper
- 4 large collard leaves, stems removed

Directions:

Combine the lentils, tomatoes, cheese, basil leaves, olive oil, vinegar, garlic, honey, salt, and black pepper and stir well.

Lay the collard leaves on a flat work surface. Spoon the equal-sized amounts of the lentil mixture onto the edges of the leaves. Roll them up and slice in half to serve.

Nutrition (for 100g): 318 Calories 17.6g Fat 27.5g Carbohydrates 13.2g Protein 800mg Sodium

Mediterranean Veggie Bowl

Preparation Time : 10 minutes

Cooking Time : 20 minutes

Servings : 4

Difficulty Level : Average

Ingredients:

- 2 cups water
- 1 cup of either bulgur wheat #3 or quinoa, rinsed
- 1½ teaspoons salt, divided
- 1-pint (2 cups) cherry tomatoes, cut in half
- 1 large bell pepper, chopped
- 1 large cucumber, chopped
- 1 cup Kalamata olives
- ½ cup freshly squeezed lemon juice
- 1 cup extra-virgin olive oil
- ½ teaspoon freshly ground black pepper

Directions:

Boil the water in a medium pot over medium heat. Add the bulgur (or quinoa) and 1 teaspoon of salt. Cover and cook for 15 to 20 minutes.

To arrange the veggies in your 4 bowls, visually divide each bowl into 5 sections. Place the cooked bulgur in one section. Follow with the tomatoes, bell pepper, cucumbers, and olives.

Scourge together the lemon juice, olive oil, remaining ½ teaspoon salt, and black pepper.

Evenly spoon the dressing over the 4 bowls. Serve immediately or cover and refrigerate for later.

Nutrition (for 100g): 772 Calories 9g Fat 6g Protein 41g Carbohydrates 944mg Sodium

Grilled Veggie and Hummus Wrap

Preparation Time : 15 minutes

Cooking Time : 10 minutes

Servings : 6

Difficulty Level : Average

Ingredients:

- 1 large eggplant
- 1 large onion
- ½ cup extra-virgin olive oil
- 1 teaspoon salt
- 6 lavash wraps or large pita bread
- 1 cup Creamy Traditional Hummus

Directions:

Preheat a grill, large grill pan, or lightly oiled large skillet on medium heat. Slice the eggplant and onion into circles. Grease the vegetables with olive oil and sprinkle with salt.

Cook the vegetables on both sides, about 3 to 4 minutes each side. To make the wrap, lay the lavash or pita flat. Lay about 2 tablespoons of hummus on the wrap.

Evenly divide the vegetables among the wraps, layering them along one side of the wrap. Gently fold over the side of the wrap with the vegetables, tucking them in and making a tight wrap.

Lay the wrap seam side-down and cut in half or thirds.

You can also wrap each sandwich with plastic wrap to help it hold its shape and eat it later.

Nutrition (for 100g): 362 Calories 10g Fat 28g Carbohydrates 15g Protein 736mg Sodium

Spanish Green Beans

Preparation Time : 10 minutes

Cooking Time : 20 minutes

Servings : 4

Difficulty Level : Easy

Ingredients:

- ¼ cup extra-virgin olive oil
- 1 large onion, chopped
- 4 cloves garlic, finely chopped
- 1-pound green beans, fresh or frozen, trimmed
- 1½ teaspoons salt, divided
- 1 (15-ounce) can diced tomatoes
- ½ teaspoon freshly ground black pepper

Directions:

Warm up the olive oil, onion, and garlic; cook for 1 minute. Cut the green beans into 2-inch pieces. Add the green beans and 1 teaspoon of salt to the pot and toss everything together; cook for 3 minutes. Add the diced tomatoes, remaining ½ teaspoon of salt, and black pepper to the pot; continue to cook for another 12 minutes, stirring occasionally. Serve warm.

Nutrition (for 100g): 200 Calories 12g Fat 18g Carbohydrates 4g Protein 639mg Sodium

Rustic Cauliflower and Carrot Hash

Preparation Time : 10 minutes

Cooking Time : 10 minutes

Servings : 4

Difficulty Level : Easy

Ingredients:

- 3 tablespoons extra-virgin olive oil
- 1 large onion, chopped
- 1 tablespoon garlic, minced
- 2 cups carrots, diced
- 4 cups cauliflower pieces, washed
- 1 teaspoon salt
- ½ teaspoon ground cumin

Directions:

Cook the olive oil, onion, garlic, and carrots for 3 minutes. Cut the cauliflower into 1-inch or bite-size pieces. Add the cauliflower, salt, and cumin to the skillet and toss to combine with the carrots and onions.

Cover and cook for 3 minutes. Toss in the vegetables and continue cooking for an additional 3 to 4 minutes. Serve warm.

Nutrition (for 100g): 159 Calories 17g Fat 15g Carbohydrates 3g Protein 569mg Sodium

Roasted Cauliflower and Tomatoes

Preparation Time : 5 minutes

Cooking Time : 25 minutes

Servings : 4

Difficulty Level : Average

Ingredients:

- 4 cups cauliflower, cut into 1-inch pieces
- 6 tablespoons extra-virgin olive oil, divided
- 1 teaspoon salt, divided
- 4 cups cherry tomatoes
- ½ teaspoon freshly ground black pepper
- ½ cup grated Parmesan cheese

Directions:

Preheat the oven to 425°F. Add the cauliflower, 3 tablespoons of olive oil, and ½ teaspoon of salt to a large bowl and toss to coat evenly. Lay onto a baking sheet in an even layer.

In another large bowl, add the tomatoes, remaining 3 tablespoons of olive oil, and ½ teaspoon of salt, and toss to coat evenly. Pour onto a different baking sheet. Put the sheet of cauliflower and the sheet of tomatoes in the oven to roast for 17 to 20 minutes until the cauliflower is lightly browned and tomatoes are plump.

Using a spatula, spoon the cauliflower into a serving dish, and top with tomatoes, black pepper, and Parmesan cheese. Serve warm.

Nutrition (for 100g): 294 Calories 14g Fat 13g Carbohydrates 9g Protein 493mg Sodium

Roasted Acorn Squash

Preparation Time : 10 minutes

Cooking Time : 35 minutes

Servings : 6

Difficulty Level : Average

Ingredients:

- 2 acorn squash, medium to large
- 2 tablespoons extra-virgin olive oil
- 1 teaspoon salt, plus more for seasoning
- 5 tablespoons unsalted butter
- ¼ cup chopped sage leaves
- 2 tablespoons fresh thyme leaves
- ½ teaspoon freshly ground black pepper

Directions:

Preheat the oven to 400°F. Cut the acorn squash in half lengthwise. Scrape out the seeds and cut it horizontally into ¾-inch-thick slices. In a large bowl, drizzle the squash with the olive oil, sprinkle with salt, and toss together to coat.

Lay the acorn squash flat on a baking sheet. Situate in the baking sheet in the oven and bake the squash for 20 minutes. Flip squash over with a spatula and bake for another 15 minutes.

Soften the butter in a medium saucepan over medium heat. Add the sage and thyme to the melted butter and let them cook for 30 seconds. Transfer the cooked squash slices to a plate. Spoon the butter/herb mixture over the squash. Season with salt and black pepper. Serve warm.

Nutrition (for 100g): 188 Calories 13g Fat 16g Carbohydrates 1g Protein 836mg Sodium

Sautéed Garlic Spinach

Preparation Time : 5 minutes
Cooking Time : 10 minutes
Servings : 4
Difficulty Level : Easy

Ingredients:

- ¼ cup extra-virgin olive oil
- 1 large onion, thinly sliced
- 3 cloves garlic, minced
- 6 (1-pound) bags of baby spinach, washed
- ½ teaspoon salt
- 1 lemon, cut into wedges

Directions:

Cook the olive oil, onion, and garlic in a large skillet for 2 minutes over medium heat. Add one bag of spinach and ½ teaspoon of salt. Cover the skillet and let the spinach wilt for 30 seconds. Repeat (omitting the salt), adding 1 bag of spinach at a time.

When all the spinach has been added in, remove the cover and cook for 3 minutes, letting some of the moisture evaporate. Serve warm with lemon zest over the top.

Nutrition (for 100g): 301 Calories 12g Fat 29g Carbohydrates 17g Protein 639mg Sodium

Garlicky Sautéed Zucchini with Mint

Preparation Time : 5 minutes
Cooking Time : 10 minutes
Servings : 4
Difficulty Level : Easy

Ingredients:

- 3 large green zucchinis
- 3 tablespoons extra-virgin olive oil
- 1 large onion, chopped
- 3 cloves garlic, minced
- 1 teaspoon salt
- 1 teaspoon dried mint

Directions:

Cut the zucchini into ½-inch cubes. Cook the olive oil, onions, and garlic for 3 minutes, stirring constantly.

Add the zucchini and salt to the skillet and toss to combine with the onions and garlic, cooking for 5 minutes. Add the mint to the skillet, tossing to combine. Cook for another 2 minutes. Serve warm.

Nutrition (for 100g): 147 Calories 16g Fat 12g Carbohydrates 4g Protein 723mg Sodium

Stewed Okra

Preparation Time : 55 minutes
Cooking Time : 25 minutes
Servings : 4
Difficulty Level : Easy

Ingredients:

- ¼ cup extra-virgin olive oil
- 1 large onion, chopped
- 4 cloves garlic, finely chopped
- 1 teaspoon salt
- 1 pound fresh or frozen okra, cleaned
- 1 (15-ounce) can plain tomato sauce
- 2 cups water
- ½ cup fresh cilantro, finely chopped
- ½ teaspoon freshly ground black pepper

Directions:

Mix and cook the olive oil, onion, garlic, and salt for 1 minute. Stir in the okra and cook for 3 minutes.

Add the tomato sauce, water, cilantro, and black pepper; stir, cover, and let cook for 15 minutes, stirring occasionally. Serve warm.

Nutrition (for 100g): 201 Calories 6g Fat 18g Carbohydrates 4g Protein 693mg Sodium

Sweet Veggie-Stuffed Peppers

Preparation Time : 20 minutes
Cooking Time : 30 minutes
Servings : 6
Difficulty Level : Average

Ingredients:

- 6 large bell peppers, different colors
- 3 tablespoons extra-virgin olive oil
- 1 large onion, chopped
- 3 cloves garlic, minced
- 1 carrot, chopped
- 1 (16-ounce) can garbanzo beans, rinsed and drained
- 3 cups cooked rice
- 1½ teaspoons salt
- ½ teaspoon freshly ground black pepper

Directions:

Preheat the oven to 350°F. Make sure to choose peppers that can stand upright. Cut off the pepper cap and remove the seeds, reserving the cap for later. Stand the peppers in a baking dish.

Warm up the olive oil, onion, garlic, and carrots for 3 minutes. Stir in the garbanzo beans. Cook for another 3 minutes. Pull out from the pan from the heat and spoon the cooked ingredients to a large bowl. Add the rice, salt, and pepper; toss to combine.

Stuff each pepper to the top and then put the pepper caps back on. Tuck the baking dish with aluminum foil and bake for 25 minutes. Pull out the foil and bake for another 5 minutes. Serve warm.

Nutrition (for 100g): 301 Calories 15g Fat 50g Carbohydrates 8g Protein 803mg Sodium

Moussaka Eggplant

Preparation Time : 55 minutes
Cooking Time : 40 minutes
Servings : 6
Difficulty Level : Difficult

Ingredients:

- 2 large eggplants
- 2 teaspoons salt, divided
- Olive oil spray
- ¼ cup extra-virgin olive oil
- 2 large onions, sliced
- 10 cloves garlic, sliced
- 2 (15-ounce) cans diced tomatoes
- 1 (16-ounce) can garbanzo beans, rinsed and drained
- 1 teaspoon dried oregano
- ½ teaspoon freshly ground black pepper

Directions:

Slice the eggplant horizontally into ¼-inch-thick round disks. Sprinkle the eggplant slices with 1 teaspoon of salt and place in a colander for 30 minutes.

Preheat the oven to 450°F. Pat the slices of eggplant dry with a paper towel and spray each side with an olive oil spray or lightly brush each side with olive oil.

Assemble the eggplant in a single layer on a baking sheet. Situate in the oven and bake for 10 minutes. Then, using a spatula, flip the slices over and bake for another 10 minutes.

Sauté the olive oil, onions, garlic, and remaining 1 teaspoon of salt. Cook 5 minutes stirring seldom. Add the tomatoes, garbanzo beans, oregano, and black pepper. Simmer for 12 minutes, stirring irregularly.

Using a deep casserole dish, begin to layer, starting with eggplant, then the sauce. Repeat until all ingredients have been used. Bake in the oven for 20 minutes. Remove from the oven and serve warm.

Nutrition (for 100g): 262 Calories 11g Fat 35g Carbohydrates 8g Protein 723mg Sodium

Vegetable-Stuffed Grape Leaves

Preparation Time : 50 minutes

Cooking Time : 45 minutes

Servings : 8

Difficulty Level : Average

Ingredients:

- 2 cups white rice, rinsed
- 2 large tomatoes, finely diced
- 1 large onion, finely chopped
- 1 green onion, finely chopped
- 1 cup fresh Italian parsley, finely chopped
- 3 cloves garlic, minced
- 2½ teaspoons salt
- ½ teaspoon freshly ground black pepper
- 1 (16-ounce) jar grape leaves
- 1 cup lemon juice
- ½ cup extra-virgin olive oil
- 4 to 6 cups water

Directions:

Combine the rice, tomatoes, onion, green onion, parsley, garlic, salt, and black pepper. Drain and rinse the grape leaves. Prepare a large pot by placing a layer of grape leaves on the bottom. Lay each leaf flat and trim off any stems.

Place 2 tablespoons of the rice mixture at the base of each leaf. Fold over the sides, then roll as tight as possible. Put the rolled grape leaves in the pot, lining up each rolled grape leaf. Continue to layer in the rolled grape leaves.

Gently pour the lemon juice and olive oil over the grape leaves, and add enough water just to cover the grape leaves by 1 inch. Lay a heavy plate that is smaller than the opening of the pot upside down over the grape leaves. Cover the pot and cook the leaves over medium-low heat for 45 minutes. Let stand for 20 minutes before serving. Serve warm or cold.

Nutrition (for 100g): 532 Calories 15g Fat 80g Carbohydrates 12g Protein 904mg Sodium

Grilled Eggplant Rolls

Preparation Time : 30 minutes

Cooking Time : 10 minutes

Servings : 6

Difficulty Level : Average

Ingredients:

- 2 large eggplants
- 1 teaspoon salt
- 4 ounces goat cheese
- 1 cup ricotta
- ¼ cup fresh basil, finely chopped
- ½ teaspoon freshly ground black pepper
- Olive oil spray

Directions:

Cut up the tops of the eggplants and cut the eggplants lengthwise into ¼-inch-thick slices. Sprinkle the slices with the salt and place the eggplant in a colander for 15 to 20 minutes.

Scourge the goat cheese, ricotta, basil, and pepper. Preheat a grill, grill pan, or lightly oiled skillet on medium heat. Pat dry the eggplant slices and lightly spray with olive oil spray. Place the eggplant on the grill, grill pan, or skillet and cook for 3 minutes on each side.

Take out the eggplant from the heat and let cool for 5 minutes. To roll, lay one eggplant slice flat, place a tablespoon of the cheese mixture at the base of the slice, and roll up. Serve immediately or chill until serving.

Nutrition (for 100g): 255 Calories 7g Fat 19g Carbohydrates 15g Protein 793mg Sodium

Crispy Zucchini Fritters

Preparation Time : 15 minutes

Cooking Time : 20 minutes

Servings : 6

Difficulty Level : Easy

Ingredients:

- 2 large green zucchinis
- 2 tablespoons Italian parsley, finely chopped
- 3 cloves garlic, minced
- 1 teaspoon salt
- 1 cup flour
- 1 large egg, beaten
- ½ cup water
- 1 teaspoon baking powder
- 3 cups vegetable or avocado oil

Directions:

Grate the zucchini into a large bowl. Add the parsley, garlic, salt, flour, egg, water, and baking powder to the bowl and stir to combine. In a large pot or fryer over medium heat, heat oil to 365°F.

Drop the fritter batter into the hot oil by spoonful. Turn the fritters over using a slotted spoon and fry until they are golden brown, about 2 to 3 minutes. Strain the fritters from the oil and place on a plate lined with paper towels. Serve warm with Creamy Tzatziki or Creamy Traditional Hummus as a dip.

Nutrition (for 100g): 446 Calories 2g Fat 19g Carbohydrates 5g Protein 812mg Sodium

Cheesy Spinach Pies

Preparation Time : 20 minutes
Cooking Time : 40 minutes
Servings : 8
Difficulty Level : Difficult

Ingredients:

- 2 tablespoons extra-virgin olive oil
- 1 large onion, chopped
- 2 cloves garlic, minced
- 3 (1-pound) bags of baby spinach, washed
- 1 cup feta cheese
- 1 large egg, beaten
- Puff pastry sheets

Directions:

Preheat the oven to 375°F. Warm up the olive oil, onion, and garlic for 3 minutes. Add the spinach to the skillet one bag at a time, letting it wilt in between each bag. Toss using tongs. Cook for 4 minutes. Once the spinach is cooked, scoop out any excess liquid from the pan.

In a large bowl, mix the feta cheese, egg, and cooked spinach. Lay the puff pastry flat on a counter. Cut the pastry into 3-inch squares. Place a tablespoon of the spinach mixture in the center of a puff-pastry square. Crease over one corner of the square to the diagonal corner, forming a triangle. Crimp the edges of the pie by pressing down with the tines of a fork to seal them together. Repeat until all squares are filled.

Situate the pies on a parchment-lined baking sheet and bake for 25 to 30 minutes or until golden brown. Serve warm or at room temperature.

Nutrition (for 100g): 503 Calories 6g Fat 38g Carbohydrates 16g Protein 836mg Sodium

Cucumber Sandwich Bites

Preparation Time : 5 minutes
Cooking Time : 0 minutes
Servings : 12
Difficulty Level : Easy

Ingredients:

- 1 cucumber, sliced
- 8 slices whole wheat bread
- 2 tablespoons cream cheese, soft
- 1 tablespoon chives, chopped
- ¼ cup avocado, peeled, pitted and mashed
- 1 teaspoon mustard
- Salt and black pepper to the taste

Directions:

Spread the mashed avocado on each bread slice, also spread the rest of the ingredients except the cucumber slices.

Divide the cucumber slices on the bread slices, cut each slice in thirds, arrange on a platter and serve as an appetizer.

Nutrition (for 100g): 187 Calories 12.4g Fat 4.5g Carbohydrates 8.2g Protein 736mg Sodium

Yogurt Dip

Preparation Time : 10 minutes
Cooking Time : 0 minutes
Servings : 6
Difficulty Level : Easy

Ingredients:

- 2 cups Greek yogurt
- 2 tablespoons pistachios, toasted and chopped
- A pinch of salt and white pepper
- 2 tablespoons mint, chopped
- 1 tablespoon kalamata olives, pitted and chopped
- ¼ cup zaatar spice
- ¼ cup pomegranate seeds
- 1/3 cup olive oil

Directions:

Mix the yogurt with the pistachios and the rest of the ingredients, whisk well, divide into small cups and serve with pita chips on the side.

Nutrition (for 100g): 294 Calories 18g Fat 2g Carbohydrates 10g Protein 593mg Sodium

Tomato Bruschetta

Preparation Time : 10 minutes

Cooking Time : 10 minutes

Servings : 6

Difficulty Level : Easy

Ingredients:

- 1 baguette, sliced
- 1/3 cup basil, chopped
- 6 tomatoes, cubed
- 2 garlic cloves, minced
- A pinch of salt and black pepper
- 1 teaspoon olive oil
- 1 tablespoon balsamic vinegar
- ½ teaspoon garlic powder
- Cooking spray

Directions:

Situate the baguette slices on a baking sheet lined with parchment paper, grease with cooking spray. Bake for 10 minutes at 400 degrees.

Combine the tomatoes with the basil and the remaining ingredients, toss well and leave aside for 10 minutes. Divide the tomato mix on each baguette slice, arrange them all on a platter and serve.

Nutrition (for 100g): 162 Calories 4g Fat 29g Carbohydrates 4g Protein 736mg Sodium

Olives and Cheese Stuffed Tomatoes

Preparation Time : 10 minutes

Cooking Time : 0 minutes

Servings : 24

Difficulty Level : Easy

Ingredients:

- 24 cherry tomatoes, top cut off and insides scooped out
- 2 tablespoons olive oil
- ¼ teaspoon red pepper flakes
- ½ cup feta cheese, crumbled
- 2 tablespoons black olive paste
- ¼ cup mint, torn

Directions:

In a bowl, mix the olives paste with the rest of the ingredients except the cherry tomatoes and whisk well. Stuff the cherry tomatoes with this mix, arrange them all on a platter and serve as an appetizer.

Nutrition (for 100g): 136 Calories 8.6g Fat 5.6g Carbohydrates 5.1g Protein 648mg Sodium

Pepper Tapenade

Preparation Time : 10 minutes
Cooking Time : 0 minutes
Servings : 4
Difficulty Level : Easy

Ingredients:

- 7 ounces roasted red peppers, chopped
- ½ cup parmesan, grated
- 1/3 cup parsley, chopped
- 14 ounces canned artichokes, drained and chopped
- 3 tablespoons olive oil
- ¼ cup capers, drained
- 1 and ½ tablespoons lemon juice
- 2 garlic cloves, minced

Directions:

In your blender, combine the red peppers with the parmesan and the rest of the ingredients and pulse well. Divide into cups and serve as a snack.

Nutrition (for 100g): 200 Calories 5.6g Fat 12.4g Carbohydrates 4.6g Protein 736mg Sodium

Coriander Falafel

Preparation Time : 10 minutes

Cooking Time : 10 minutes

Servings : 8

Difficulty Level : Easy

Ingredients:

- 1 cup canned garbanzo beans
- 1 bunch parsley leaves
- 1 yellow onion, chopped
- 5 garlic cloves, minced
- 1 teaspoon coriander, ground
- A pinch of salt and black pepper
- ¼ teaspoon cayenne pepper
- ¼ teaspoon baking soda
- ¼ teaspoon cumin powder
- 1 teaspoon lemon juice
- 3 tablespoons tapioca flour
- Olive oil for frying

Directions:

In your food processor, combine the beans with the parsley, onion and the rest the ingredients except the oil and the flour and pulse well. Transfer the mix to a bowl, add the flour, stir well, shape 16 balls out of this mix and flatten them a bit.

Preheat pan over medium-high heat, add the falafels, cook them for 5 minutes on both sides, put in paper towels, drain excess grease, arrange them on a platter and serve as an appetizer.

Nutrition (for 100g): 122 Calories 6.2g Fat 12.3g Carbohydrates 3.1g Protein 699mg Sodium

Red Pepper Hummus

Preparation Time : 10 minutes
Cooking Time : 0 minutes
Servings : 6
Difficulty Level : Easy

Ingredients:

- 6 ounces roasted red peppers, peeled and chopped
- 16 ounces canned chickpeas, drained and rinsed
- ¼ cup Greek yogurt
- 3 tablespoons tahini paste
- Juice of 1 lemon
- 3 garlic cloves, minced
- 1 tablespoon olive oil
- A pinch of salt and black pepper
- 1 tablespoon parsley, chopped

Directions:

In your food processor, combine the red peppers with the rest of the ingredients except the oil and the parsley and pulse well. Add the oil, pulse again, divide into cups, sprinkle the parsley on top and serve as a party spread.

Nutrition (for 100g): 255 Calories 11.4g Fat 17.4g Carbohydrates 6.5g Protein 593mg Sodium

White Bean Dip

Preparation Time : 10 minutes
Cooking Time : 0 minutes
Servings : 4
Difficulty Level : Easy

Ingredients:

- 15 ounces canned white beans, drained and rinsed
- 6 ounces canned artichoke hearts, drained and quartered
- 4 garlic cloves, minced
- 1 tablespoon basil, chopped
- 2 tablespoons olive oil
- Juice of ½ lemon
- Zest of ½ lemon, grated
- Salt and black pepper to the taste

Directions:

In your food processor, combine the beans with the artichokes and the rest of the ingredients except the oil and pulse well. Add the oil gradually, pulse the mix again, divide into cups and serve as a party dip.

Nutrition (for 100g): 27 Calories 11.7g Fat 18.5g Carbohydrates 16.5g Protein 668mg Sodium

Hummus with Ground Lamb

Preparation Time : 10 minutes

Cooking Time : 15 minutes

Servings : 8

Difficulty Level : Easy

Ingredients:

- 10 ounces hummus
- 12 ounces lamb meat, ground
- ½ cup pomegranate seeds
- ¼ cup parsley, chopped
- 1 tablespoon olive oil
- Pita chips for serving

Directions:

Preheat pan over medium-high heat, cook the meat, and brown for 15 minutes stirring often. Spread the hummus on a platter, spread the ground lamb all over, also spread the pomegranate seeds and the parsley and serve with pita chips as a snack.

Nutrition (for 100g): 133 Calories 9.7g Fat 6.4g Carbohydrates 5.4g Protein 659mg Sodium

Eggplant Dip

Preparation Time : 10 minutes
Cooking Time : 40 minutes
Servings : 4
Difficulty Level : Easy

Ingredients:

- 1 eggplant, poked with a fork
- 2 tablespoons tahini paste
- 2 tablespoons lemon juice
- 2 garlic cloves, minced
- 1 tablespoon olive oil
- Salt and black pepper to the taste
- 1 tablespoon parsley, chopped

Directions:

Put the eggplant in a roasting pan, bake at 400 degrees F for 40 minutes, cool down, peel and transfer to your food processor. Blend the rest of the ingredients except the parsley, pulse well, divide into small bowls and serve as an appetizer with the parsley sprinkled on top.

Nutrition (for 100g): 121 Calories 4.3g Fat 1.4g Carbohydrates 4.3g Protein 639mg Sodium

Veggie Fritters

Preparation Time : 10 minutes
Cooking Time : 10 minutes
Servings : 8
Difficulty Level : Easy

Ingredients:

- 2 garlic cloves, minced
- 2 yellow onions, chopped
- 4 scallions, chopped
- 2 carrots, grated
- 2 teaspoons cumin, ground
- ½ teaspoon turmeric powder
- Salt and black pepper to the taste
- ¼ teaspoon coriander, ground
- 2 tablespoons parsley, chopped
- ¼ teaspoon lemon juice
- ½ cup almond flour
- 2 beets, peeled and grated
- 2 eggs, whisked
- ¼ cup tapioca flour
- 3 tablespoons olive oil

Directions:

In a bowl, combine the garlic with the onions, scallions and the rest of the ingredients except the oil, stir well and shape medium fritters out of this mix.

Preheat pan over medium-high heat, place the fritters, cook for 5 minutes on each side, arrange on a platter and serve.

Nutrition (for 100g): 209 Calories 11.2g Fat 4.4g Carbohydrates 4.8g Protein 726mg Sodium

Bulgur Lamb Meatballs

Preparation Time : 10 minutes
Cooking Time : 15 minutes
Servings : 6
Difficulty Level : Easy

Ingredients:

- 1 and ½ cups Greek yogurt
- ½ teaspoon cumin, ground
- 1 cup cucumber, shredded
- ½ teaspoon garlic, minced
- A pinch of salt and black pepper
- 1 cup bulgur
- 2 cups water
- 1-pound lamb, ground
- ¼ cup parsley, chopped
- ¼ cup shallots, chopped
- ½ teaspoon allspice, ground
- ½ teaspoon cinnamon powder
- 1 tablespoon olive oil

Directions:

Mix the bulgur with the water, cover the bowl, leave aside for 10 minutes, drain and transfer to a bowl. Add the meat, the yogurt and the rest of the ingredients except the oil, stir well and shape medium meatballs out of this mix. Preheat pan over medium-high heat, place the meatballs, cook them for 7 minutes on each side, arrange them all on a platter and serve as an appetizer.

Nutrition (for 100g): 300 Calories 9.6g Fat 22.6g Carbohydrates 6.6g Protein 644mg Sodium

Cucumber Bites

Preparation Time : 10 minutes

Cooking Time : 0 minutes

Servings : 12

Difficulty Level : Easy

Ingredients:

- 1 English cucumber, sliced into 32 rounds
- 10 ounces hummus
- 16 cherry tomatoes, halved
- 1 tablespoon parsley, chopped
- 1-ounce feta cheese, crumbled

Directions:

Spread the hummus on each cucumber round, divide the tomato halves on each, sprinkle the cheese and parsley on to and serve as an appetizer.

Nutrition (for 100g): 162 Calories 3.4g Fat 6.4g Carbohydrates 2.4g Protein 702mg Sodium

Stuffed Avocado

Preparation Time : 10 minutes

Cooking Time : 0 minutes

Servings : 2

Difficulty Level : Easy

Ingredients:

- 1 avocado, halved and pitted
- 10 ounces canned tuna, drained
- 2 tablespoons sun-dried tomatoes, chopped
- 1 and ½ tablespoon basil pesto
- 2 tablespoons black olives, pitted and chopped
- Salt and black pepper to the taste
- 2 teaspoons pine nuts, toasted and chopped
- 1 tablespoon basil, chopped

Directions:

Mix the tuna with the sun-dried tomatoes and the rest of the ingredients except the avocado and stir. Stuff the avocado halves with the tuna mix and serve as an appetizer.

Nutrition (for 100g): 233 Calories 9g Fat 11.4g Carbohydrates 5.6g Protein 735mg Sodium

Wrapped Plums

Preparation Time : 5 minutes
Cooking Time : 0 minutes
Servings : 8
Difficulty Level : Easy

Ingredients:

- 2 ounces prosciutto, cut into 16 pieces
- 4 plums, quartered
- 1 tablespoon chives, chopped
- A pinch of red pepper flakes, crushed

Directions:

Wrap each plum quarter in a prosciutto slice, arrange them all on a platter, sprinkle the chives and pepper flakes all over and serve.

Nutrition (for 100g): 30 Calories 1g Fat 4g Carbohydrates 2g Protein 439mg Sodium

Marinated Feta and Artichokes

Preparation Time : 10 minutes, plus 4 hours inactive time
Cooking Time : 10 minutes
Servings : 2
Difficulty Level : Easy

Ingredients:

- 4 ounces traditional Greek feta, cut into ½-inch cubes
- 4 ounces drained artichoke hearts, quartered lengthwise
- 1/3 cup extra-virgin olive oil
- Zest and juice of 1 lemon
- 2 tablespoons roughly chopped fresh rosemary
- 2 tablespoons roughly chopped fresh parsley
- ½ teaspoon black peppercorns

Directions:

In a glass bowl combine the feta and artichoke hearts. Add the olive oil, lemon zest and juice, rosemary, parsley, and peppercorns and toss gently to coat, being sure not to crumble the feta.

Cool for 4 hours, or up to 4 days. Take out of the refrigerator 30 minutes before serving.

Nutrition (for 100g): 235 Calories 23g Fat 1g Carbohydrates 4g Protein 714mg Sodium

Tuna Croquettes

Preparation Time : 40 minutes, plus hours to overnight to chill
Cooking Time : 25 minutes
Servings : 36
Difficulty Level : Difficult

Ingredients:

- 6 tablespoons extra-virgin olive oil, plus 1 to 2 cups
- 5 tablespoons almond flour, plus 1 cup, divided
- 1¼ cups heavy cream
- 1 (4-ounce) can olive oil-packed yellowfin tuna
- 1 tablespoon chopped red onion
- 2 teaspoons minced capers
- ½ teaspoon dried dill
- ¼ teaspoon freshly ground black pepper
- 2 large eggs
- 1 cup panko breadcrumbs (or a gluten-free version)

Directions:

In a large skillet, warm up 6 tablespoons olive oil over medium-low heat. Add 5 tablespoons almond flour and cook, stirring constantly, until a smooth paste forms and the flour browns slightly, 2 to 3 minutes.

Select the heat to medium-high and gradually mix in the heavy cream, whisking constantly until completely smooth and thickened, another 4 to 5 minutes. Remove and add in the tuna, red onion, capers, dill, and pepper.

Transfer the mixture to an 8-inch square baking dish that is well coated with olive oil and set aside at room temperature. Wrap and cool for 4 hours or up to overnight. To form the croquettes, set out three bowls. In one, beat together the eggs. In another, add the remaining almond flour. In the third, add the panko. Line a baking sheet with parchment paper.

Scoop about a tablespoon of cold prepared dough into the flour mixture and roll to coat. Shake off excess and, using your hands, roll into an oval.

Dip the croquette into the beaten egg, then lightly coat in panko. Set on lined baking sheet and repeat with the remaining dough.

In a small saucepan, warm up the remaining 1 to 2 cups of olive oil, over medium-high heat.

Once the oil is heated, fry the croquettes 3 or 4 at a time, depending on the size of your pan, removing with a slotted spoon when golden brown. You will need to adjust the temperature of the oil occasionally to prevent burning. If the croquettes get dark brown very quickly, lower the temperature.

Nutrition (for 100g): 245 Calories 22g Fat 1g Carbohydrates 6g Protein 801mg Sodium

Smoked Salmon Crudités

Preparation Time : 10 minutes

Cooking Time : 15 minutes

Servings : 4

Difficulty Level : Easy

Ingredients:

- 6 ounces smoked wild salmon
- 2 tablespoons Roasted Garlic Aioli
- 1 tablespoon Dijon mustard
- 1 tablespoon chopped scallions, green parts only
- 2 teaspoons chopped capers
- ½ teaspoon dried dill
- 4 endive spears or hearts of romaine
- ½ English cucumber, cut into ¼-inch-thick rounds

Directions:

Roughly cut the smoked salmon and transfer in a small bowl. Add the aioli, Dijon, scallions, capers, and dill and mix well. Top endive spears and cucumber rounds with a spoonful of smoked salmon mixture and enjoy chilled.

Nutrition (for 100g): 92 Calories 5g Fat 1g Carbohydrates 9g Protein 714mg Sodium

Citrus-Marinated Olives

Preparation Time : 4 hours

Cooking Time : 0 minutes

Servings : 2

Difficulty Level : Easy

Ingredients:

- 2 cups mixed green olives with pits
- ¼ cup red wine vinegar
- ¼ cup extra-virgin olive oil
- 4 garlic cloves, finely minced
- Zest and juice of 1 large orange
- 1 teaspoon red pepper flakes
- 2 bay leaves
- ½ teaspoon ground cumin
- ½ teaspoon ground allspice

Directions:

Incorporate the olives, vinegar, oil, garlic, orange zest and juice, red pepper flakes, bay leaves, cumin, and allspice and mix well. Seal and chill for 4 hours or up to a week to allow the olives to marinate, tossing again before serving.

Nutrition (for 100g): 133 Calories 14g Fat 2g Carbohydrates 1g Protein 714mg Sodium

Olive Tapenade with Anchovies

Preparation Time : 1hour and 10 minutes

Cooking Time : 0 minutes

Servings : 2

Difficulty Level : Average

Ingredients:

- 2 cups pitted Kalamata olives or other black olives
- 2 anchovy fillets, chopped
- 2 teaspoons chopped capers
- 1 garlic clove, finely minced
- 1 cooked egg yolk
- 1 teaspoon Dijon mustard
- ¼ cup extra-virgin olive oil
- Seedy Crackers, Versatile Sandwich Round, or vegetables, for serving (optional)

Directions:

Rinse the olives in cold water and drain well. In a food processor, blender, or a large jar (if using an immersion blender) place the drained olives, anchovies, capers, garlic, egg yolk, and Dijon. Process until it forms a thick paste. While running, gradually stream in the olive oil.

Handover to a small bowl, cover, and refrigerate at least 1 hour to let the flavors develop. Serve with Seedy Crackers, atop a Versatile Sandwich Round, or with your favorite crunchy vegetables.

Nutrition (for 100g): 179 Calories 19g Fat 2g Carbohydrates 2g Protein 82mg Sodium

Greek Deviled Eggs

Preparation Time : 45 minutes

Cooking Time : 15 minutes

Servings : 4

Difficulty Level : Easy

Ingredients:

- 4 large hardboiled eggs
- 2 tablespoons Roasted Garlic Aioli
- ½ cup finely crumbled feta cheese
- 8 pitted Kalamata olives, finely chopped
- 2 tablespoons chopped sun-dried tomatoes
- 1 tablespoon minced red onion
- ½ teaspoon dried dill
- ¼ teaspoon freshly ground black pepper

Directions:

Chop the hardboiled eggs in half lengthwise, remove the yolks, and place the yolks in a medium bowl. Reserve the egg white halves and set aside. Smash the yolks well with a fork. Add the aioli, feta, olives, sun-dried tomatoes, onion, dill, and pepper and stir to combine until smooth and creamy.

Spoon the filling into each egg white half and chill for 30 minutes, or up to 24 hours, covered.

Nutrition (for 100g): 147 Calories 11g Fat 6g Carbohydrates 9g Protein 736mg Sodium

Manchego Crackers

Preparation Time : 1hour and 15 minutes

Cooking Time : 15 minutes

Servings : 20

Difficulty Level : Difficult

Ingredients:

- 4 tablespoons butter, at room temperature
- 1 cup finely shredded Manchego cheese
- 1 cup almond flour
- 1 teaspoon salt, divided
- ¼ teaspoon freshly ground black pepper
- 1 large egg

Directions:

Using an electric mixer, scourge together the butter and shredded cheese until well combined and smooth. Incorporate the almond flour with ½ teaspoon salt and pepper. Gradually put the almond flour mixture to the cheese, mixing constantly until the dough just comes together to form a ball.

Situate a piece of parchment or plastic wrap and roll into a cylinder log about 1½ inches thick. Seal tightly then freeze for at least 1 hour. Preheat the oven to 350°F. Put parchment paper or silicone baking mats into 2 baking sheets.

To make the egg wash, scourge together the egg and remaining ½ teaspoon salt. Slice the refrigerated dough into small rounds, about ¼ inch thick, and place on the lined baking sheets.

Egg wash the tops of the crackers and bake until the crackers are golden and crispy. Situate on a wire rack to cool.

Serve warm or, once fully cooled, store in an airtight container in the refrigerator for up to 1 week.

Nutrition (for 100g): 243 Calories 23g Fat 1g Carbohydrates 8g Protein 804mg Sodium

Burrata Caprese Stack

Preparation Time: 5 minutes
Cooking Time: 0 minutes
Servings: 4
Difficulty Level: Easy

Ingredients:

- 1 large organic tomato, preferably heirloom
- ½ teaspoon salt
- ¼ teaspoon freshly ground black pepper
- 1 (4-ounce) ball burrata cheese
- 8 fresh basil leaves, thinly sliced
- 2 tablespoons extra-virgin olive oil
- 1 tablespoon red wine or balsamic vinegar

Directions:

Slice the tomato into 4 thick slices, removing any tough center core and sprinkle with salt and pepper. Place the tomatoes, seasoned-side up, on a plate. On a separate rimmed plate, slice the burrata into 4 thick slices and place one slice on top of each tomato slice. Top each with one-quarter of the basil and pour any reserved burrata cream from the rimmed plate over top.

Dash with olive oil and vinegar and serve with a fork and knife.

Nutrition (for 100g): 153 Calories 13g Fat 1g Carbohydrates 7g Protein 633mg Sodium

Zucchini-Ricotta Fritters with Lemon-Garlic Aioli

Preparation Time : 10 minutes, plus 20 minutes rest time
Cooking Time : 25 minutes
Servings : 4
Difficulty Level : Difficult

Ingredients:

- 1 large or 2 small/medium zucchini
- 1 teaspoon salt, divided
- ½ cup whole-milk ricotta cheese
- 2 scallions
- 1 large egg
- 2 garlic cloves, finely minced
- 2 tablespoons chopped fresh mint (optional)
- 2 teaspoons grated lemon zest
- ¼ teaspoon freshly ground black pepper
- ½ cup almond flour
- 1 teaspoon baking powder
- 8 tablespoons extra-virgin olive oil
- 8 tablespoons Roasted Garlic Aioli or avocado oil mayonnaise

Directions:

Situate the shredded zucchini in a colander or on several layers of paper towels. Sprinkle with ½ teaspoon salt and let sit for 10 minutes. Using another layer of paper towel press down on the zucchini to release any excess moisture and pat dry. Incorporate the drained zucchini, ricotta, scallions, egg, garlic, mint (if using), lemon zest, remaining ½ teaspoon salt, and pepper.

Scourge together the almond flour and baking powder. Fold in the flour mixture into the zucchini mixture and let rest for 10 minutes. In a large skillet, working in four batches, fry the fritters. For each batch of four, heat 2 tablespoons olive oil over medium-high heat. Add 1 heaping tablespoon of zucchini batter per fritter, pressing down with the back of a spoon to form 2- to 3-inch fritters. Cover and let fry 2 minutes before flipping. Fry another 2 to 3 minutes, covered, or until crispy and golden and cooked through. You may need to reduce heat to medium to prevent burning. Remove from the pan and keep warm.

Repeat for the remaining three batches, using 2 tablespoons of the olive oil for each batch. Serve fritters warm with aioli.

Nutrition (for 100g): 448 Calories 42g Fat 2g Carbohydrates 8g Protein 744mg Sodium

Salmon-Stuffed Cucumbers

Preparation Time : 10 minutes
Cooking Time : 0 minutes
Servings : 4
Difficulty Level : Easy

Ingredients:

- 2 large cucumbers, peeled
- 1 (4-ounce) can red salmon
- 1 medium very ripe avocado
- 1 tablespoon extra-virgin olive oil
- Zest and juice of 1 lime
- 3 tablespoons chopped fresh cilantro
- ½ teaspoon salt
- ¼ teaspoon freshly ground black pepper

Directions:

Slice the cucumber into 1-inch-thick segments and using a spoon, scrape seeds out of center of each segment and stand up on a plate. In a medium bowl, mix the salmon, avocado, olive oil, lime zest and juice, cilantro, salt, and pepper and mix until creamy.

Scoop the salmon mixture into the center of each cucumber segment and serve chilled.

Nutrition (for 100g): 159 Calories 11g Fat 3g Carbohydrates 9g Protein 739mg Sodium

Goat Cheese–Mackerel Pâté

Preparation Time : 10 minutes

Cooking Time : 0 minutes

Servings : 4

Difficulty Level : Easy

Ingredients:

- 4 ounces olive oil-packed wild-caught mackerel
- 2 ounces goat cheese
- Zest and juice of 1 lemon
- 2 tablespoons chopped fresh parsley
- 2 tablespoons chopped fresh arugula
- 1 tablespoon extra-virgin olive oil
- 2 teaspoons chopped capers
- 1 to 2 teaspoons fresh horseradish (optional)
- Crackers, cucumber rounds, endive spears, or celery, for serving (optional)

Directions:

In a food processor, blender, or large bowl with immersion blender, combine the mackerel, goat cheese, lemon zest and juice, parsley, arugula, olive oil, capers, and horseradish (if using). Process or blend until smooth and creamy.

Serve with crackers, cucumber rounds, endive spears, or celery. Seal covered in the refrigerator for up to 1 week.

Nutrition (for 100g): 118 Calories 8g Fat 6g Carbohydrates 9g Protein 639mg Sodium

Taste of the Mediterranean Fat Bombs

Preparation Time : 4hours and 15 minutes

Cooking Time : 0 minutes

Servings : 6

Difficulty Level : Average

Ingredients:

- 1 cup crumbled goat cheese
- 4 tablespoons jarred pesto
- 12 pitted Kalamata olives, finely chopped
- ½ cup finely chopped walnuts
- 1 tablespoon chopped fresh rosemary

Directions:

In a medium bowl, scourge the goat cheese, pesto, and olives and mix well using a fork. Freeze for 4 hours to toughen.

With your hands, create the mixture into 6 balls, about ¾-inch diameter. The mixture will be sticky.

In a small bowl, place the walnuts and rosemary and roll the goat cheese balls in the nut mixture to coat. Store the fat bombs in the refrigerator for up to 1 week or in the freezer for up to 1 month.

Nutrition (for 100g): 166 Calories 15g Fat 1g Carbohydrates 5g Protein 736mg Sodium

Avocado Gazpacho

Preparation Time : 15 minutes

Cooking Time : 10 minutes

Servings : 4

Difficulty Level : Easy

Ingredients:

- 2 cups chopped tomatoes
- 2 large ripe avocados, halved and pitted
- 1 large cucumber, peeled and seeded
- 1 medium bell pepper (red, orange or yellow), chopped
- 1 cup plain whole-milk Greek yogurt
- ¼ cup extra-virgin olive oil
- ¼ cup chopped fresh cilantro
- ¼ cup chopped scallions, green part only
- 2 tablespoons red wine vinegar
- Juice of 2 limes or 1 lemon
- ½ to 1 teaspoon salt
- ¼ teaspoon freshly ground black pepper

Directions:

Using an immersion blender, combine the tomatoes, avocados, cucumber, bell pepper, yogurt, olive oil, cilantro, scallions, vinegar, and lime juice. Blend until smooth.

Season and blend to combine the flavors. Serve cold.

Nutrition (for 100g): 392 Calories 32g Fat 9g Carbohydrates 6g Protein 694mg Sodium

Crab Cake Lettuce Cups

Preparation Time : 35 minutes

Cooking Time : 20 minutes

Servings : 4

Difficulty Level : Average

Ingredients:

- 1-pound jumbo lump crab
- 1 large egg
- 6 tablespoons Roasted Garlic Aioli
- 2 tablespoons Dijon mustard
- ½ cup almond flour
- ¼ cup minced red onion
- 2 teaspoons smoked paprika
- 1 teaspoon celery salt
- 1 teaspoon garlic powder
- 1 teaspoon dried dill (optional)
- ½ teaspoon freshly ground black pepper
- ¼ cup extra-virgin olive oil
- 4 large Bibb lettuce leaves, thick spine removed

Directions:

Situate the crabmeat in a large bowl and pick out any visible shells, then break apart the meat with a fork. In a small bowl, scourge together the egg, 2 tablespoons aioli, and Dijon mustard. Add to the crabmeat and blend with a fork. Add the almond flour, red onion, paprika, celery salt, garlic powder, dill (if using), and pepper and combine well. Allow rest at room temperature for 10 to 15 minutes.

Form into 8 small cakes, about 2 inches in diameter. Cook the olive oil over medium-high heat. Fry the cakes until browned, 2 to 3 minutes per side. Wrap, decrease the heat to low, and cook for another 6 to 8 minutes, or until set in the center. Remove from the skillet.

To serve, wrap 2 small crab cakes in each lettuce leaf and top with 1 tablespoon aioli.

Nutrition (for 100g): 344 Calories 24g Fat 2g Carbohydrates 24g Protein 804mg Sodium

Orange-Tarragon Chicken Salad Wrap

Preparation Time : 15 minutes

Cooking Time : 0 minutes

Servings : 4

Difficulty Level : Easy

Ingredients:

- ½ cup plain whole-milk Greek yogurt
- 2 tablespoons Dijon mustard
- 2 tablespoons extra-virgin olive oil
- 2 tablespoons fresh tarragon
- ½ teaspoon salt
- ¼ teaspoon freshly ground black pepper
- 2 cups cooked shredded chicken
- ½ cup slivered almonds
- 4 to 8 large Bibb lettuce leaves, tough stem removed
- 2 small ripe avocados, peeled and thinly sliced
- Zest of 1 clementine, or ½ small orange (about 1 tablespoon)

Directions:

In a medium bowl, mix the yogurt, mustard, olive oil, tarragon, orange zest, salt, and pepper and whisk until creamy. Add the shredded chicken and almonds and stir to coat.

To assemble the wraps, place about ½ cup chicken salad mixture in the center of each lettuce leaf and top with sliced avocados.

Nutrition (for 100g): 440 Calories 32g l Fat 8g Carbohydrates 26g Protein 607mg Sodium

Feta and Quinoa Stuffed Mushrooms

Preparation Time : 5 minutes

Cooking Time : 8 minutes

Servings : 6

Difficulty Level : Average

Ingredients:

- 2 tablespoons finely diced red bell pepper
- 1 garlic clove, minced
- ¼ cup cooked quinoa
- 1/8 teaspoon salt
- ¼ teaspoon dried oregano
- 24 button mushrooms, stemmed
- 2 ounces crumbled feta
- 3 tablespoons whole wheat bread crumbs
- Olive oil cooking spray

Directions:

Preheat the air fryer to 360°F. In a small bowl, mix the bell pepper, garlic, quinoa, salt, and oregano. Spoon the quinoa stuffing into the mushroom caps until just filled. Add a small piece of feta to the top of each mushroom. Sprinkle a pinch bread crumbs over the feta on each mushroom.

Put the basket of the air fryer with olive oil cooking spray, then gently place the mushrooms into the basket, making sure that they don't touch each other.

Lay the basket into the air fryer and bake for 8 minutes. Remove from the air fryer and serve.

Nutrition (for 100g): 97 Calories 4g Fat 11g Carbohydrates 7g Protein 677mg Sodium

Five-Ingredient Falafel with Garlic-Yogurt Sauce

Preparation Time : 5 minutes

Cooking Time : 15 minutes

Servings : 4

Difficulty Level : Difficult

Ingredients:

- <u>For the falafel</u>
- 1 (15-ounce) can chickpeas, drained and rinsed
- ½ cup fresh parsley
- 2 garlic cloves, minced
- ½ tablespoon ground cumin
- 1 tablespoon whole wheat flour
- Salt
- <u>For the garlic-yogurt sauce</u>
- 1 cup nonfat plain Greek yogurt
- 1 garlic clove, minced
- 1 tablespoon chopped fresh dill
- 2 tablespoons lemon juice

Directions:

To make the falafel

Preheat the air fryer to 360°F. Put the chickpeas into a food processor. Pulse until mostly chopped, then add the parsley, garlic, and cumin and pulse for another minutes, until the ingredients turn into a dough.

Add the flour. Pulse a few more times until combined. The dough will have texture, but the chickpeas should be pulsed into small bits. Using clean hands, roll the dough into 8 balls of equal size, then pat the balls down a bit so they are about ½-thick disks.

Put the basket of the air fryer with olive oil cooking spray, then place the falafel patties in the basket in a single layer, making sure they don't touch each other. Fry in the air fryer for 15 minutes.

To make the garlic-yogurt sauce

Mix the yogurt, garlic, dill, and lemon juice. Once the falafel is done cooking and nicely browned on all sides, remove them from the air fryer and season with salt. Serve hot side it dipping sauce.

Nutrition (for 100g): 151 Calories 2g Fat 10g Carbohydrates 12g Protein 698mg Sodium

Lemon Shrimp with Garlic Olive Oil

Preparation Time : 5minutes

Cooking Time : 6 minutes

Servings : 4

Difficulty Level : Average

Ingredients:

- 1-pound medium shrimp, cleaned and deveined
- ¼ cup plus 2 tablespoons olive oil, divided
- Juice of ½ lemon
- 3 garlic cloves, minced and divided
- ½ teaspoon salt
- ¼ teaspoon red pepper flakes
- Lemon wedges, for serving (optional)
- Marinara sauce, for dipping (optional)

Directions:

Preheat the air fryer to 380°F. Toss in the shrimp with 2 tablespoons of the olive oil, lemon juice, 1/3 of minced garlic, salt, and red pepper flakes and coat well.

In a small ramekin, combine the remaining ¼ cup of olive oil and the remaining minced garlic. Tear off a 12-by-12-inch sheet of aluminum foil. Place the shrimp into the center of the foil, then fold the sides up and crimp the edges so that it forms an aluminum foil bowl that is open on top. Place this packet into the air fryer basket.

Roast the shrimp for 4 minutes, then open the air fryer and place the ramekin with oil and garlic in the basket beside the shrimp packet. Cook for 2 more minutes. Transfer the shrimp on a serving plate or platter with the ramekin of garlic olive oil on the side for dipping. You may also serve with lemon wedges and marinara sauce, if desired.

Nutrition (for 100g): 264 Calories 21g Fat 10g Carbohydrates 16g Protein 473mg Sodium

Crispy Green Bean Fries with Lemon-Yogurt Sauce

Preparation Time : 5 minutes
Cooking Time : 5 minutes
Servings : 4
Difficulty Level : Average

Ingredients:

- <u>For the green beans</u>
- 1 egg
- 2 tablespoons water
- 1 tablespoon whole wheat flour
- ¼ teaspoon paprika
- ½ teaspoon garlic powder
- ½ teaspoon salt
- ¼ cup whole wheat bread crumbs
- ½ pound whole green beans
- <u>For the lemon-yogurt sauce</u>
- ½ cup nonfat plain Greek yogurt
- 1 tablespoon lemon juice
- ¼ teaspoon salt
- 1/8 teaspoon cayenne pepper

Direction:

To make the green beans

Preheat the air fryer to 380°F.

In a medium shallow bowl, combine together the egg and water until frothy. In a separate medium shallow bowl, whisk together the flour, paprika, garlic powder, and salt, then mix in the bread crumbs.

Spread the bottom of the air fryer with cooking spray. Dip each green bean into the egg mixture, then into the bread crumb mixture, coating the outside with the crumbs. Situate the green beans in a single layer in the bottom of the air fryer basket.

Fry in the air fryer for 5 minutes, or until the breading is golden brown.

To make the lemon-yogurt sauce

Incorporate the yogurt, lemon juice, salt, and cayenne. Serve the green bean fries alongside the lemon-yogurt sauce as a snack or appetizer.

Nutrition (for 100g): 88 Calories 2g Fat 10g Carbohydrates 7g Protein 697mg Sodium

Homemade Sea Salt Pita Chips

Preparation Time : 2 minutes
Cooking Time : 8 minutes
Servings : 2
Difficulty Level : Easy

Ingredients:

- 2 whole wheat pitas
- 1 tablespoon olive oil
- ½ teaspoon kosher salt

Directions

Preheat the air fryer to 360°F. Cut each pita into 8 wedges. In a medium bowl, mix the pita wedges, olive oil, and salt until the wedges are coated and the olive oil and salt are evenly distributed.

Place the pita wedges into the air fryer basket in an even layer and fry for 6 to 8 minutes.

Season with additional salt, if desired. Serve alone or with a favorite dip.

Nutrition (for 100g): 230 Calories 8g Fat 11g Carbohydrates 6g Protein 810mg Sodium

Baked Spanakopita Dip

Preparation Time : 10 minutes

Cooking Time : 15 minutes

Servings : 2

Difficulty Level : Average

Ingredients:

- Olive oil cooking spray
- 3 tablespoons olive oil, divided
- 2 tablespoons minced white onion
- 2 garlic cloves, minced
- 4 cups fresh spinach
- 4 ounces cream cheese, softened
- 4 ounces feta cheese, divided
- Zest of 1 lemon
- ¼ teaspoon ground nutmeg
- 1 teaspoon dried dill
- ½ teaspoon salt
- Pita chips, carrot sticks, or sliced bread for serving (optional)

Directions:

Preheat the air fryer to 360°F. Coat the inside of a 6-inch ramekin or baking dish with olive oil cooking spray.

In a large skillet over medium heat, heat 1 tablespoon of the olive oil. Add the onion, then cook for 1 minute. Add in the garlic and cook, stirring for 1 minute more.

Lower heat and combine the spinach and water. Cook until the spinach has wilted. Remove the skillet from the heat. In a medium bowl, scourge the cream cheese, 2 ounces of the feta, and the rest of olive oil, lemon zest, nutmeg, dill, and salt. Mix until just combined.

Add the vegetables to the cheese base and stir until combined. Pour the dip mixture into the prepared ramekin and top with the remaining 2 ounces of feta cheese.

Place the dip into the air fryer basket and cook for 10 minutes, or until heated through and bubbling. Serve with pita chips, carrot sticks, or sliced bread.

Nutrition (for 100g): 550 Calories 52g Fat 21g Carbohydrates 14g Protein 723mg Sodium

Roasted Pearl Onion Dip

Preparation Time : 5 minutes

Cooking Time : 12 minutes plus 1 hour to chill

Servings : 4

Difficulty Level : Average

Ingredients:

- 2 cups peeled pearl onions
- 3 garlic cloves
- 3 tablespoons olive oil, divided
- ½ teaspoon salt
- 1 cup nonfat plain Greek yogurt
- 1 tablespoon lemon juice
- ¼ teaspoon black pepper
- 1/8 teaspoon red pepper flakes
- Pita chips, vegetables, or toasted bread for serving (optional)

Directions:

Preheat the air fryer to 360°F. In a large bowl, combine the pearl onions and garlic with 2 tablespoons of the olive oil until the onions are well coated.

Pour the garlic-and-onion mixture into the air fryer basket and roast for 12 minutes. Place the garlic and onions to a food processor. Pulse the vegetables several times, until the onions are minced but still have some chunks.

Toss in the garlic and onions and the remaining 1 tablespoon of olive oil, along with the salt, yogurt, lemon juice, black pepper, and red pepper flakes. Chill for 1 hour before serving with pita chips, vegetables, or toasted bread.

Nutrition (for 100g): 150 Calories 10g Fat 6g Carbohydrates 7g Protein 693mg Sodium

Red Pepper Tapenade

Preparation Time : 5 minutes

Cooking Time : 5 minutes

Servings : 4

Difficulty Level : Average

Ingredients:

- 1 large red bell pepper
- 2 tablespoons plus 1 teaspoon olive oil
- ½ cup Kalamata olives, pitted and roughly chopped
- 1 garlic clove, minced
- ½ teaspoon dried oregano
- 1 tablespoon lemon juice

Directions:

Preheat the air fryer to 380°F. Brush the outside of a whole red pepper with 1 teaspoon olive oil and place it inside the air fryer basket. Roast for 5 minutes. For the meantime, in a medium bowl incorporate the remaining 2 tablespoons of olive oil with the olives, garlic, oregano, and lemon juice.

Remove the red pepper from the air fryer, then gently slice off the stem and remove the seeds. Roughly chop the roasted pepper into small pieces.

Add the red pepper to the olive mixture and stir all together until combined. Serve with pita chips, crackers, or crusty bread.

Nutrition (for 100g): 104 Calories 10g Fat 9g Carbohydrates 1g Protein 644mg Sodium

Greek Potato Skins with Olives and Feta

Preparation Time : 5 minutes

Cooking Time : 45 minutes

Servings : 4

Difficulty Level : Difficult

Ingredients:

- 2 russet potatoes
- 3 tablespoons olive oil
- 1 teaspoon kosher salt, divided
- ¼ teaspoon black pepper
- 2 tablespoons fresh cilantro
- ¼ cup Kalamata olives, diced
- ¼ cup crumbled feta
- Chopped fresh parsley, for garnish (optional)

Directions:

Preheat the air fryer to 380°F. Using a fork, poke 2 to 3 holes in the potatoes, then coat each with about ½ tablespoon olive oil and ½ teaspoon salt.

Situate the potatoes into the air fryer basket and bake for 30 minutes. Remove the potatoes from the air fryer, and slice in half. Scrape out the flesh of the potatoes using a spoon, leaving a ½-inch layer of potato inside the skins, and set the skins aside.

In a medium bowl, combine the scooped potato middles with the remaining 2 tablespoons of olive oil, ½ teaspoon of salt, black pepper, and cilantro. Mix until well combined. Divide the potato filling into the now-empty potato skins, spreading it evenly over them. Top each potato with a tablespoon each of the olives and feta.

Place the loaded potato skins back into the air fryer and bake for 15 minutes. Serve with additional chopped cilantro or parsley and a drizzle of olive oil, if desired.

Nutrition (for 100g): 270 Calories 13g Fat 34g Carbohydrates 5g Protein 672mg Sodium

Artichoke and Olive Pita Flatbread

Preparation Time : 5 minutes

Cooking Time : 10 minutes

Servings : 4

Difficulty Level : Easy

Ingredients:

- 2 whole wheat pitas
- 2 tablespoons olive oil, divided
- 2 garlic cloves, minced
- ¼ teaspoon salt
- ½ cup canned artichoke hearts, sliced
- ¼ cup Kalamata olives
- ¼ cup shredded Parmesan
- ¼ cup crumbled feta
- Chopped fresh parsley, for garnish (optional)

Directions:

Preheat the air fryer to 380°F. Brush each pita with 1 tablespoon olive oil, then sprinkle the minced garlic and salt over the top.

Distribute the artichoke hearts, olives, and cheeses evenly between the two pitas, and place both into the air fryer to bake for 10 minutes. Remove the pitas and cut them into 4 pieces each before serving. Sprinkle parsley over the top, if desired.

Nutrition (for 100g): 243 Calories 15g Fat 10g Carbohydrates 7g Protein 644mg Sodium

Mini Crab Cakes

Preparation Time : 10 minutes
Cooking Time : 10 minutes
Servings : 6
Difficulty Level : Average

Ingredients:

- 8 ounces lump crab meat
- 2 tablespoons diced red bell pepper
- 1 scallion, white parts and green parts, diced
- 1 garlic clove, minced
- 1 tablespoon capers, minced
- 1 tablespoon nonfat plain Greek yogurt
- 1 egg, beaten
- ¼ cup whole wheat bread crumbs
- ¼ teaspoon salt
- 1 tablespoon olive oil
- 1 lemon, cut into wedges

Directions:

Preheat the air fryer to 360°F. In a medium bowl, mix the crab, bell pepper, scallion, garlic, and capers until combined. Add the yogurt and egg. Stir until incorporated. Mix in the bread crumbs and salt.

Portion this mixture into 6 equal parts and pat out into patties. Place the crab cakes inside the air fryer basket on single layer, separately. Grease the tops of each patty with a bit of olive oil. Bake for 10 minutes.

Remove the crab cakes from the air fryer and serve with lemon wedges on the side.

Nutrition (for 100g): 87 Calories 4g Fat 6g Carbohydrates 9g Protein 574mg Sodium

Zucchini Feta Roulades

Preparation Time : 10 minutes

Cooking Time : 10 minutes

Servings : 6

Difficulty Level : Average

Ingredients:

- ½ cup feta
- 1 garlic clove, minced
- 2 tablespoons fresh basil, minced
- 1 tablespoon capers, minced
- 1/8 teaspoon salt
- 1/8 teaspoon red pepper flakes
- 1 tablespoon lemon juice
- 2 medium zucchinis
- 12 toothpicks

Directions:

Preheat the air fryer to 360°F. (If using a grill attachment, make sure it is inside the air fryer during preheating.) In a small bowl, mix the feta, garlic, basil, capers, salt, red pepper flakes, and lemon juice.

Slice the zucchini into 1/8-inch strips lengthwise. (Each zucchini should yield around 6 strips.) Spread 1 tablespoon of the cheese filling onto each slice of zucchini, then roll it up and locked it with a toothpick through the middle.

Place the zucchini roulades into the air fryer basket in a one layer, individually. Bake or grill in the air fryer for 10 minutes. Remove the zucchini roulades from the air fryer and gently remove the toothpicks before serving.

Nutrition (for 100g): 46 Calories 3g Fat 6g Carbohydrates 3g Protein 710mg Sodium

CPSIA information can be obtained
at www.ICGtesting.com
Printed in the USA
LVHW080311090822
725492LV00007B/130